REGENTS RENAISSANCE

General Editor: Cyr

Advisory Editor: G. .

A

Books are to be returned on or before
the last date below

LIBREX —

JOHN MARSTON

Antonio and Mellida
THE FIRST PART

Edited by

G. K. HUNTER

LONDON
EDWARD ARNOLD (PUBLISHERS) LTD.

Printed in Great Britain by
William Clowes and Sons, Limited, London and Beccles

Regents Renaissance Drama Series

The purpose of the Regents Renaissance Drama Series is to provide soundly edited texts, in modern spelling, of the more significant plays of the Elizabethan, Jacobean, and Caroline theater. Each text in the series is based on a fresh collation of all sixteenth- and seventeenth-century editions. The textual notes, which appear above the line at the bottom of each page, record all substantive departures from the edition used as the copy-text. Variant substantive readings among sixteenth- and seventeenth-century editions are listed there as well. In cases where two or more of the old editions present widely divergent readings, a list of substantive variants in editions through the seventeenth century is given in an appendix. Editions after 1700 are referred to in the textual notes only when an emendation originating in some one of them is received into the text. Variants of accidentals (spelling, punctuation, capitalization) are not recorded in the notes. Contracted forms of characters' names are silently expanded in speech prefixes and stage directions, and, in the case of speech prefixes, are regularized. Additions to the stage directions of the copy-text are enclosed in brackets. Stage directions such as "within" or "aside" are enclosed in parentheses when they occur in the copy-text.

Spelling has been modernized along consciously conservative lines. "Murther" has become "murder," and "burthen," "burden," but within the limits of a modernized text, and with the following exceptions, the linguistic quality of the original has been carefully preserved. The variety of contracted forms (*'em, 'am, 'm, 'um, 'hem*) used in the drama of the period for the pronoun *them* are here regularly given as *'em*, and the alternation between *a'th'* and *o'th'* (for *on* or *of the*) is regularly reproduced as *o'th'*. The copy-text distinction between preterite endings in *-d* and *-ed* is preserved except where the elision of *e* occurs in the penultimate syllable; in such cases, the final syllable is contracted. Thus, where the old editions read "threat'ned," those of the present series read "threaten'd." Where, in the old editions, a contracted preterite in *-y'd* would yield *-i'd* in modern spelling (as in "try'd," "cry'd," "deny'd"), the word is here given in its full form (e.g., "tried," "cried," "denied").

-v-

Punctuation has been brought into accord with modern practices. The effort here has been to achieve a balance between the generally light pointing of the old editions, and a system of punctuation which, without overloading the text with exclamation marks, semicolons, and dashes, will make the often loosely flowing verse (and prose) of the original syntactically intelligible to the modern reader. Dashes are regularly used only to indicate interrupted speeches, or shifts of address within a single speech.

Explanatory notes, chiefly concerned with glossing obsolete words and phrases, are printed below the textual notes at the bottom of each page. References to stage directions in the notes follow the admirable system of the Revels editions, whereby stage directions are keyed, decimally, to the line of the text before or after which they occur. Thus, a note on 0.2 has reference to the second line of the stage direction at the beginning of the scene in question. A note on 115.1 has reference to the first line of the stage direction following line 115 of the text of the relevant scene.

CYRUS HOY

University of Rochester

Contents

Abbreviations

Q	*The History of Antonio and Mellida; The First Part.* 1602.
1633	*The Workes of Mr. John Marston.* 1633.
Halliwell	J. O. Halliwell, ed. *The Works of John Marston.* London, 1856.
Bullen	A. H. Bullen, ed. *The Works of John Marston.* London, 1887.
S.D.	Stage direction
S.P.	Speech prefix
Tilley	Morris Palmer Tilley. *A Dictionary of the Proverbs in England in the Sixteenth and Seventeenth Centuries.* Ann Arbor, 1950.

Introduction

TEXT

The first mention of *Antonio and Mellida*—I refer by this title to only the "First Part" (here printed)—appears in the Stationers' Register, where it was entered, together with the "Second Part," *Antonio's Revenge*, on October 24, 1601:

> Ent. M. Lownes and T. Fysher (provided lawful licence is obtained): a booke called the fyrst and second partes of the play called Anthonio and Melida (single fee).

We may assume that the book was published early in the following year; the date 1602 appears on all known title pages. That to the "First Part" reads as follows:

> The history of Antonio and Mellida. The first part. As it hath beene sundry times acted, by the children of Paules. Written by I.M. [device 321] London ¶ Printed for Mathewe Lownes, and Thomas Fisher, and are to be soulde in Saint Dunstans Church-yarde. 1602.

The text contained in this quarto is a good one; even the Latin and Italian passages are well printed, by Elizabethan standards. The texts of the songs are missing, but this is no evidence of corruption; song-texts are of a distinct category from play-texts. The stage directions are Latinate and literary; much space is devoted to the description of elaborate entries, but theatrically important exits are sometimes omitted. This suggests that the "copy" behind the quarto printing did not come from the playhouse. All the evidence suggests a manuscript carefully prepared for the press and aiming at the appearance of a literary and even classical document. We must suppose that Marston himself was responsible for the preparation.

DATE

A terminal date for the two parts of *Antonio and Mellida* is provided by the entry in the Stationers' Register (quoted above) on October 24, 1601. The title page tells us that the play was acted by the children of

Paul's, and the nature of the text assures us that it was written for the child-actors; the children had been prevented from acting from *c.* 1590 till 1599. Therefore the play cannot be before 1599. The reminiscence of Sylvester's Du Bartas at line 58 of the Induction (if it be allowed) indicates that the writing comes after 1598. It has been thought that a more exact date is provided by that passage in which Balurdo examines two pictures, one marked *"Anno Domini* 1599" and the other *"Aetatis suae* 24" (V.i. 7 ff.). Marston was christened on October 7, 1576; he was, therefore, only twenty-two years old for most of 1599. But he was, after October, 1599, in the "twenty-fourth year of his age," and the coincidence of the two figures, "1599" and "24," seems too strong to allow us to reject this dating for the play. McGinn and Caputi, however, would prefer a later date: Caputi supposes *Jack Drum's Entertainment* (clearly 1600) to precede *Antonio and Mellida.* The evidence, however, seems to be rather weak. Certainly I cannot accept the common view that the reference to summer in the prologue to *Antonio and Mellida* and to winter in the prologue of *Antonio's Revenge* means that these plays were written for production in summer and winter. The Paul's theater was enclosed and lit by artificial light; the references are in fact to the climates of the two plays, to the masks of comedy and tragedy. We might as well seek to prove from the opening lines of Shakespeare's *Richard III* that it was written for production in the early summer.

The complicated relationship of *Antonio's Revenge* to Shakespeare's *Hamlet* has an obvious bearing on the dating of the double play; but the uncertainty about the different versions of *Hamlet* makes it impossible to use Shakespeare's play as a guidepost. I shall discuss the problem of this relationship in the preface to *Antonio's Revenge.*

SOURCES AND IMITATIONS

No single source for *Antonio and Mellida* has ever been discovered; indeed the structure of the play seems to express too aptly the alternation between philosophically endured deprivation and the frivolity of power—one of the recurrent themes of Marston's satire—to have originated anywhere outside the mind of its author. The play is, nonetheless, a tissue of scraps and attitudes taken from other authors. Marston's stoicism, like that of other Elizabethans, was heavily indebted to the rhetoric of Seneca, who had expressed with memorable concision the extreme states of passion, fury, jealousy, despair, which the stoic doctrine was designed to cope with; quotations from Seneca's plays abound throughout *Antonio and Mellida*, in both Latin and English. The figure of Andrugio seems, however, to be closer to the English versions of stoical endurance in extremity, especially to Hieronimo and Titus Andronicus, the famous grieved and deprived stage fathers of an earlier generation.

In disguising his hero as an Amazon, and so giving him an immediate, though rather embarrassing, intimacy with the Princess he loves, Marston seems to have remembered Sidney's *Arcadia*; in this, Pyrocles woos the Princess of his choice while disguised as an Amazon. That the connection was in Marston's mind would seem to be indicated by a verbal reminiscence (I.i.23 ff.), in Antonio's storm-description, of the famous conceit in Pyrocles' shipwreck—"their blood had (as it were) filled the wrinkles of the sea's visage." The concluding device of the play may also come from the *Arcadia*. Andrugio comes to his enemy's court to claim the reward offered for Andrugio's head; similarly, in the story of the Paphlagonian unkind king (*Arcadia*, Bk. II, cap. x) Plexirtus

> having gotten a passport for one (that pretended he would put Plexirtus alive into his hands) to speak with the King his brother, he himself . . . with a rope about his neck, barefooted, came to offer himself to the discretion of Leonatus.
>
> (Feuillerat, I.213)

The scenes of courtly frivolity in *Antonio and Mellida* have many reminiscences of Marston's own satires. In his handling of the dialogue of witty and musical pages he is obviously indebted to the theatrical tradition of which John Lyly was the acknowledged master.

Marston makes no attempt to amalgamate or reconcile these disparate elements, drawn from a wide variety of sources. Indeed he seems anxious to keep the strong contrasts between court and country, frivolity and philosophy, love and hate, as clear-cut as possible. He seems to be less interested in a coherent narrative than in the system of contrasts which the story illustrates. In a typically brilliant perception T. S. Eliot notes that Marston's poetic drama is pervaded by "doubleness in the action":

> He is . . . occupied in saying something else than appears in the literal actions and characters whom he manipulates.
>
> (*Selected Essays*, p. 229)

Elsewhere, Eliot says of Marston's *Sophonisba*:

> As we familiarize ourselves with the play we perceive a pattern behind the pattern, into which the characters deliberately involve themselves. (*ibid.* p. 232)

It is my endeavor in the critical essay below to consider *Antonio and Mellida* primarily in terms of this "figure in the carpet."

THE PLAY

A summary of the plot of *Antonio and Mellida* makes it sound like a repetitive farrago of all the silliest elements known to Elizabethan drama. Characters veer from insensate stupidity to diabolical cunning without warning and apparently without cause; attitudes are assumed and dropped at the merest whim of the author; situations are laboriously built up and then abandoned. It is as well that the interest of Marston and of the reader is not required to rest entirely on this ramshackle structure; it may be supposed that Marston's real interests lay elsewhere, and it is to this area that we must direct our attention when we read *Antonio and Mellida*.

This point should be clear right from the beginning of the play. Antonio's opening soliloquy gives us the basic narrative facts: he and his father, who

> Would with an armed hand have seiz'd thy love
> And link'd thee to the beauteous Mellida,

have been defeated in a sea battle by Piero, Duke of Venice and father to Mellida. But it is not the human situation thus organized, but rather the mood of the opening speech that is impressive:

> Heart, wilt not break? And thou, abhorred life,
> Wilt thou still breathe in my enraged blood?
> Veins, sinews, arteries, why crack ye not,
> Burst and divuls'd with anguish of my grief?
> Can man by no means creep out of himself
> And leave the slough of viperous grief behind?

And it is this mood (of greater grief than human flesh can bear) that is caught up in the following episode (of opposite outlook), and so on in alternations throughout the play. Antonio's despair, Andrugio's nobility, Piero's *hubris*, Feliche's stoical detachment—these provide the "figure in the carpet" which gives the play its basic interest, matching despair, or rather desperation, against the "Babel pride" which scorns human limits; love is set against detachment, the wise man's detachment against the fool's detachment, and so on.

It would seem to be this pattern that has to be invoked if we wish to justify, or even explain, the comic episodes which take up so much space in the play—a little less than half the total number of lines. These farcical scenes of court folly cannot be seen as foisted into a work which would be complete enough without them. The romantic story of Antonio's love for Mellida, which carries the characters through "the comic crosses of true love," is not, in fact, as important for what I have described as the basic pattern of the play as are these scenes of inane comedy, which document the background of both Folly and Pride. Courtly fawning in Castilio and Forobosco, empty-headed power in Matzagente and Galeatzo, female affectation in Rossaline and Flavia, and a more comprehensive folly in Balurdo (the thing itself)—these provide an image of the "social whirl" which is both bewildering and inane, a tribute to power which is both comforting and contemptible, explaining Andrugio's loneliness, Piero's sense of having arrived, and Feliche's disgust. These scenes are also genuinely amusing, like thumbnail jestbook sketches:

ROSSALINE.
 Foh, what a strong scent's here! somebody useth to wear socks.
BALURDO.
 By this fair candlelight 'tis not my feet. I never wore socks since I suck'd pap.
ROSSALINE.
 Savorly put off.   (II.i.55–59)

We should notice how much the furibund author of *The Scourge of Villainy* has modified his "satyric" rage in presenting the court life of *Antonio and Mellida*. A comparison with the very similar episodes in Jonson's *Cynthia's Revels* reveals Marston's genuine gift for comedy—a gift too often overlooked in this play through a primary interest in the revenge themes of the "Second Part," *Antonio's Revenge*.

But we misunderstand the comedy of *Antonio and Mellida*, as we misunderstand all the aspects of the play, if we try to isolate them from the total structure. Nor can we plot any process of organic growth out of one attitude into another. This is, indeed, a kind of relationship which Marston seems anxious to deny. What he seems to see most clearly (and asks us to see with him) are the discontinuities, the disappointments, the sudden reversals of fortune, the ironies of a complex human situation. Thus one obvious value in the play is that of stoical fortitude; but Marston cannot leave this without criticism. Feliche must be intended to be taken seriously, and his praise of stoical content (III.ii.42 ff.) is both morally exalted and poetically beautiful; but Marston immediately follows this paean by a scene in which the fine sentiments are undercut by Feliche's patent inability to support them. Moreover, Marston seems anxious to undercut nobility by the basest instrument available—in this case the fake gallant Castilio, with his love letter written to himself; even he is enough to break down the grave measures of stoical self-sufficiency:

FELICHE.
    Confusion seize me, but I think thou liest.
    . . . methinks I am as like a man.
    Troth! I have a good head of hair, a check
    Not as yet wan'd, a leg, faith, in the full.   (III.ii.68–72)

Similarly Marston places Andrugio's noble description of the true prince (IV.i.46 ff.) immediately before an exchange in which the pose of *apatheia* is betrayed into passionate involvement:

ANDRUGIO.
    Name not the Genoese; that very word
    Unkings me quite, makes me vile passion's slave.
                         (IV.i.68–69)

We cannot suppose that these juxtapositions are accidental.

Critics have, on the whole, taken Marston's betrayals of nobility as a betrayal of his art. Certainly Lamb's unqualified praise for the noble sentiments cannot be sustained, for the play will not sustain what the speeches seem to say, when considered as anthology pieces. But I would argue that the play is not intended to sustain them; in the betrayal lies the art. The separate attitudes are no more intended to be taken alone than are the separate voices of medieval polyphony. What Marston is interested in is not the way that one attitude forms itself out of another, but how one collapses to reveal the unexpected coexistence of another (coexistence, need I add, involving no need for cooperation). The plot is constructed as an extraordinary series of reversals, unprepared transitions from one level of experience to another (lower) one. Reversal is not here, however, associated with the other Aristotelian virtue—*anagnorisis*, or recognition. The plot provides numerous opportunities for the characters to discover what kind of people they are in fact (Piero a tyrant, Matzagente a windbag, Forobosco a parasite); but Marston explicitly avoids any hint of self-knowledge or even of any "real" selves. The characters remain entirely flat, and their virtue is to be easily manipulable functions of a many-leveled and ironic structure (irony operating here as a kind of compressed reversal, existing independent of plot development). The *volte-face* between Part One and Part Two has been much commented on as a sign of Marston's change of intention; but it is no more unprepared than the many *voltes-face* in *Antonio and Mellida* itself.

The view of "character" that I have presented here should be linked to the fact that *Antonio and Mellida* was written to be acted by boys, not by men. The companies of choir boys, who had provided courtly entertainment throughout the Tudor period, and "private" performances for a select audience since 1576, had been prevented from performing for the last ten years or so of the sixteenth century. They reopened their theaters about 1599, probably with some of their old repertory (dating from the eighties), but these plays seem to have been hissed at as

> mouldy fopperies of stale poetry
> Unpossible dry musty fictions,

as Marston himself calls them in *Jack Drum's Entertainment*. The new times demanded a new taste in drama, and new authors like Marston and Ben Jonson were quick to substitute plays like *Cynthia's Revels* and *Antonio and Mellida* for those of the older mode. Both these plays resemble the earlier boys' plays (those of John Lyly, for example) by being concerned with court manners; but they define these in terms of a new sharp-edged satiric vision, set against an ideal of stoical disengagement. The pattern of inane court manners is acted out by puppets who are completely unaware of themselves, but the play makes sure that we in the audience shall not remain equally unaware. This puppet-action was ideally suited to the talents of the boys. So far as we can tell, their gifts were in short tableau-like presentations of action, in ensemble and quick-change contrasts. They could have had little power of overwhelming their audiences by the magnetic projection of personality.

Marston seems to show, in *Antonio and Mellida*, a close acquaintance with Shakespeare's *Richard III* and *Richard II*; but he makes no attempt to follow Shakespeare by centering his action on a single, fully delineated character. His choice of another mode need not be regarded, however, as inherent weakness. At the very least it can be seen as showing an awareness of the nature of his instruments—the children of St. Paul's. But, more than this, we should see that the disparity between the child-actor and the adult role is a powerful means of presenting the meaningful artificiality of the play-world, and insisting on a dramatic vision of life with its own (non-Shakespearean) force and validity. The *Inductions* of Jonson and Marston obviously ask for a Pirandello-like awareness of the play-world deliberately made unreal. In *Antonio and Mellida* we begin with the players, discussing among themselves the roles they must shortly assume. We learn not only that the boys are distinct from their roles, but that the roles themselves belong to theatrical stock:

FELICHE.
    Rampum scrampum, mount tufty Tamburlaine! What
    rattling thunderclap breaks from his lips?
ALBERTO.
    O, 'tis native to his part. For acting a modern Bragadoch
    under the person of Matzagente, the Duke of Milan's son, it
    may seem to suit with good fashion of coherence.
                                                    (Ind., 86 ff.)

As in Pirandello, the characters' lack of self-knowledge is ironically pointed to by a structure which presents this as symptomatic of the whole human condition.

Those who have pointed to the elements just discussed have usually seen the discontinuities between the boy-players and their roles as due to weakness rather than deliberation. One must welcome, therefore, the recent suggestion, made independently by Anthony Caputi and R. A. Foakes, that *Antonio and Mellida* is deliberately guying the passionate style of plays designed for adult companies. It is supposed that when the passionate speeches of *Antonio and Mellida* were spoken by children they would appear absurd to the sophisticated audience of the playhouse "in Paul's." The greatest disadvantage of this view is that it operates within an intolerably coarse-grained view of "parody." There is no space here to attempt to define what parody could have meant to the Elizabethans; but even a modern audience entirely innocent of historical knowledge should be aware that parody involves more than humor. Modern parodies, such as Terence Rattigan's *Variations on a Theme* (based on *La Dame aux Camélias*) or Picasso's variations on Velasquez' *Meninas*, should remind us that the war horses of the past can be "parodied" without any suggestion that we should laugh at them.

Marston was certainly exploiting the "passionate" style as an already established mode; and he was certainly conscious of the discrepancy between the boys' natural range and the texture he was asking them to work in. But the clash of opposites can produce more than comedy. *Antonio and Mellida* asks us to see the matter of court intrigue as at once passionately serious and absurdly pointless; and there is no good ground for supposing that Marston thought one of these viewpoints more basic than the other. A modern play like *Waiting for Godot* should remind us that the tragic and the absurd may belong together. Indeed Marston showed a taste for these bizarre conjunctions, even from his earliest writings. The double vision of his *Metamorphosis of Pigmalion's Image*, at once erotic and anti-erotic, and the mode of his satires—fascinated by what they attack—demonstrate a characteristic ambivalence of outlook which makes Marston one of the strangest as well as one of the most modern of the Elizabethans.

The central difficulty with Marston is a stylistic difficulty; and the problems of appreciating *Antonio and Mellida* that I have already mentioned are most sharply focused when seen in relation to the style in which the play is written. Historical awareness offers us no help here; Marston's style was seen as barbarous by his own contemporaries. Ben Jonson brought him on the stage in *Poetaster,* and there administered him a pill to bring up all the hard words he had swallowed, words like *glibbery, lubrical, snotteries, turgidous,* etc. In the Parnassus Plays, acted in Cambridge about 1601, he appears as Furor Poeticus, and in the last of the three plays he is "censured," under his own name, as

> . . . a ruffian in his style
> Withouten bands or garter's ornament
> . . . Brings the great battering-ram of terms to town.
> (ed. Leishman, ll. 269 ff.)

It is clear enough that the faults of style which we notice today were no less obvious to Marston's contemporaries. Nonetheless, the classical and academic standards of "good writing" by which Marston stands condemned have their limitations. Jonson is admitted to be narrow and partisan when he condemns Shakespeare; and we may see that Marston had a different view of dramatic language from that of his detractors. It is one of Marston's reiterated critical points that the life of drama lies in theatrical performance; and some at least of the oddities of his expression can be explained as attempts to communicate his vision in terms which would be theatrically expressive, even if not valuable as book-literature.

His vision of life (which I have already discussed) was one which stressed the incapacity of any single attitude to sustain itself against the bitter ironies of incessant betrayal. Marston's satire is essentially something which feeds on rejection—a rejection which was comprehensive enough to include the ground on which the rejector himself stood. Even in his ostensibly nondramatic poems he is nearly always speaking through a persona, which at some moments he seems to have felt to be repulsive or absurd and presented as such. In stylistic terms this means a lack of any settled norm of language or tone of voice which we can accept as "proper"; the clash of extremes (which is what we find in his style) can be seen on this count to be an inevitable part of his vision. This is not to prove it good, of course—an intention to write badly is no defence—but we should probably argue in terms other than those of mere incapacity.

Marston saw the world as a place where nobility is forever lapsing into caricature, and communication forever betraying intention. In terms of dramatic language this means a breakdown in the rhetoric of persuasion by which one character controls another (e.g., Richard III and the Lady Anne). Marston uses many devices obviously designed to catch the incoherence of real speech, real attempts to communicate, really obstructed by the separateness of individual temperaments. An instructive example of this in the play before us can be seen at V.i.67 ff., where the opening lines indicate the indirection:

FELICHE.
> Now, Master Balurdo, whither are you going, ha?

BALURDO.
> Signior Feliche, how do you, faith, and by my troth, how do you?

FELICHE.
> Whither art thou going, bully?

BALURDO.

And as heaven help me, how do you? How do you i' faith,
hee?

FELICHE.

Whither art going, man?

The lack of communication here between the Stoic and the courtling
is aptly represented by a conversation which proceeds entirely on
lines of crossed connections, each speaker out of touch with the other.
The admirers of the modern "theatre of the absurd" (Ionesco,
Beckett, Pinter, Albee) will notice how modern Marston is here.

Marston's fondness for *aposiopesis* (sudden breaks in speech) can be
seen as part of the same effort to render the real and (in his view)
significant incoherence of speech. He sees passion as leading not to
action but inaction, not only to eloquence but also to inarticulateness:

O, this is naught but speckling melancholy.
I have been—
That Morpheus tender skinp—Cousin german—
Bear with me good—
Mellida—Clod upon clod thus fall.
Hell is beneath; yet Heaven is over all.

(IV.i.24–29)

Aposiopesis is used sometimes to suggest the inability of some
characters to keep up with the standards of style they have set for
themselves. Elsewhere it is a means of delineating the mind that tries
to hold two objects in view at one time, speaking about one and
pursuing the other; there are excellent examples of this in the
flattering speeches of Flavia and Forobosco:

By your sweet self,
than whom I know not a more exquisite, illustrate, accom-
plished, pure, respected, ador'd, observed, precious, real,
magnanimous, bounteous—if you have an idle rich cast
jerkin or so, it shall not be cast away, if—Ha! here's a
forehead, an eye, a head, a hair that would make a—or if
you have any spare pair of silver spurs . . . .

(II.i.109–115)

Allied to aposiopesis in their power to reduce speech to mere
ejaculation are the many repetitions and exclamatory noises with
which the play is studded: "with a pah! 'slid . . ." (II.i.8), or "Whop!

Fut . . ." (II.i.107). Even the climactic moment when Mellida is recaptured is expressed in this way:

BALURDO.

God's neaks, proud elf, give the Duke reverence; stand bare, with a—[*Knocks her cap off.*] Whogh! Heavens bless me— Mellida, Mellida!

(IV.i.242–244)

The continuity of style on which literary effect depends is broken down by the combination of these and similar devices.

But Marston's aim is not to be satisfied by any mere approximation to the incoherence of real-life dialogue. The effects he aims at are poetic, though not book-literary; he aims to awaken our response to situations by the *words* he uses and not by our sense of the people who speak them. Take the situation in Act III, Scene ii (ll. 262 ff.), the situation surrounding Piero's palindrome:

> Fly, call, run, row, ride, cry, shout, hurry, haste;
> Haste, hurry, shout, cry, ride, row, run, call, fly;
> Backward and forward, every way about.

Here it is the order of words that is meant to awaken our response to the meaning. An extraordinary richness of verbal orchestration is obviously aimed at throughout this passage. The breakdown of Piero's ironically presented *hubris* is managed by a gradual increase of tempo throughout the exchange with Flavia. This is set against the non-involvement of Feliche, represented by his song (which is a list of great men undone by love), while the Italian couplet serves, like a motto under an emblem, to pose the whole action as in a tableau. The power of continuity is weak here, and in consequence the text is not easy to *read*, but the skill in counterpoint is sufficient to carry the scene, if we allow separate voices for the separate effects. This effort to represent the discontinuous variousness of experience is clearly what lies behind Marston's drastic use of Italian and Latin, culminating in the twenty-line passage of Italian in IV.i, when the two lovers find themselves together and apparently out of danger. What Marston seems to have been aiming at here was a love-strain more remote from everyday conversation than anything he could achieve in English. The stilted Petrarchisms of the opera-like dialogue are clearly meant to counterpoint the base vernacular confusions of the surrounding search and the crass common sense of the page, whose comment follows immediately.

Marston's very extensive use of music in the play should be seen in the same context. Music was, of course, an essential part of the entertainment in the boys' theaters. What is interesting here is the extent to which the play requires music to make it complete; the statuesque scenes, the simplified characterization, the emotions on stilts—all these point forward to that acceptable form of absurdity we call opera. The emotions expressed in *Antonio and Mellida* stand apart from one another much as do the arias of the older operatic style. The serious personal expressions which we find are, like the serious emotions of *Don Giovanni* or *The Marriage of Figaro*, at a reach beyond the ordinary business of living which surrounds them, in an area of self-sufficient poetry; the rest of the world touches this only in parody, as comment from another and completely separate plane of existence (Leporello under the table while the trombones summon his master to Hell). Such analogies seem very remote; but it is to them rather than to any ideal of the "well-made play" that we should look if we wish to understand the form of *Antonio and Mellida*.

The editor wishes to thank Mr. E. Dawson for the emendation recorded at IV.i.205.

G. K. Hunter

University of Liverpool

ANTONIO AND MELLIDA

[Names of the Actors

Andrugio, *lately Duke of Genoa*
Antonio, *his son*
Lucio, *his counselor*
Page *to Andrugio*
Piero Sforza, *Duke of Venice*   5
Feliche
Balurdo
Alberto   } *Gentlemen of Piero's court.*
Castilio Balthazar
Forobosco   10
Catzo, *page to Castilio*
Dildo, *page to Balurdo*
Galeatzo, *son to the Duke of Florence*
Matzagente, *son to the Duke of Milan*
A Painter   15

Mellida, *daughter to Piero*
Flavia, *her gentlewoman*
Rossaline, *her cousin*
Three Pages]

---

5. *Piero Sforza*] probably to be associated with Lodovico Sforza, Duke of Milan, conventionalized as an "Italianate" tyrant.
6. *Feliche*] phonetic rendering of *Felice*, "the happy man."
7. *Balurdo*] "a fool, a noddy, a dizzard, an idiot, a giddy head" (Florio's Italian dictionary [1598]).
9. *Castilio Balthazar*] Balthazar Castiglione was the famous author of *The Courtier.*
10. *Forobosco*] "A bird called a woodpecker. Also a sneaking, prying, busy fellow" (Florio).
11. *Catzo*] "a man's privy member" (Florio)—used derisively for a person.
12. *Dildo*] ditto.
14. *Matzagente*] "a killer or queller of people, a man-queller" (Florio).

To the only rewarder, and most just poiser of virtuous merits, the most honorably renowned Nobody, bounteous Maecenas of Poetry and Lord Protector of oppressed innocence, *Do, Dedicoque.*

Since it hath flow'd with the current of my humorous 5
blood to affect (a little too much) to be seriously fantastical,
here take (most respected Patron) the worthless present of
my slighter idleness. If you vouchsafe not his protection, then,
O thou sweetest perfection, female beauty, shield me from
the stopping of vinegar bottles. Which most wished favor if 10
it fail me, then *Si nequeo flectere superos, Acheronta movebo.* But
yet, honor's redeemer, virtue's advancer, religion's shelter
and piety's fosterer, yet, yet, I faint not in despair of thy
gracious affection and protection; to which I only shall
ever rest most servingman-like, obsequiously making legs 15
and standing, after our freeborn English garb, bareheaded.
Thy only affied slave and admirer,

J.M.

---

1. *poiser*] weigher.
2. *Maecenas*] patron.
4. *Do, Dedicoque*] "I give, and dedicate (this work)."
5. *humorous*] moody.
8. *slighter*] rather unimportant.
8. *his protection*] the protection of my work.
10. *stopping*] unstoppering.
10. *vinegar bottles*] (1) bitterness, satire; (2) treatment for pox.
11. *Si . . . movebo*] "If I cannot bend the Gods to my will, I will work on the infernal powers." A standard tag, here slightly altered, from Virgil *Aeneid* (vii) 312.
15. *making legs*] bowing in deference.
16. *bareheaded*] (1) without a hat (not possessing one); (2) with doffed hat (out of reverence).
17. *affied*] assured.

Induction

Enter Galeatzo, Piero, Alberto, Antonio, Forobosco, Balurdo, Matzagente *and* Feliche, *with parts in their hands, having cloaks cast over their apparel.*

GALEATZO.

    Come sirs, come! the music will sound straight for entrance.
    Are ye ready, are ye perfect?

PIERO.

    Faith, we can say our parts; but we are ignorant in what
    mold we must cast our actors.

ALBERTO.

    Whom do you personate?   5

PIERO.

    Piero, Duke of Venice.

ALBERTO.

    O, ho; then thus frame your exterior shape
    To haughty form of elate majesty
    As if you held the palsy-shaking head
    Of reeling chance under your fortune's belt   10
    In strictest vassalage; grow big in thought
    As swoll'n with glory of successful arms.

PIERO.

    If that be all, fear not, I'll suit it right.
    Who cannot be proud, stroke up the hair and strut?

ALBERTO.

    Truth. Such rank custom is grown popular;   15
    And now the vulgar fashion strides as wide
    And stalks as proud upon the weakest stilts
    Of the slight'st fortunes as if Hercules
    Or burly Atlas shoulder'd up their state.

PIERO.

    Good. But whom act you?   20

ALBERTO.

    The necessity of the play forceth me to act two parts,
    Andrugio the distressed Duke of Genoa, and Alberto a
    Venetian gentleman enamored on the Lady Rossaline,

1. S.P. GALEATZO] *1633; not in Q.*

---

8. *elate*] elevated.

whose fortunes being too weak to sustain the port of her, he
prov'd always disastrous in love, his worth being much   25
underpoised by the uneven scale that currents all things by
the outward stamp of opinion.

GALEATZO.

Well, and what dost thou play?

BALURDO.

The part of all the world.

ALBERTO.

The part of all the world? What's that?   30

BALURDO.

The fool. Ay, in good deed, la, now I play Balurdo, a
wealthy mountebanking Burgomasco's heir of Venice.

ALBERTO.

Ha, ha; one whose foppish nature might seem create only
for wise men's recreation, and like a juiceless bark, to
preserve the sap of more strenuous spirits. A servile hound   35
that loves the scent of forerunning fashion; like an empty
hollow vault still giving an echo to wit, greedily champing
what any other well-valued judgment had beforehand
chew'd.

FOROBOSCO.

Ha, ha, ha; tolerably good; good, faith, sweet wag.   40

ALBERTO.

Umph; why "tolerably good; good, faith, sweet wag"?
Go, go; you flatter me.

FOROBOSCO.

Right; I but dispose my speech to the habit of my part.

ALBERTO [*to* Feliche].

Why, what plays he?

33. create] *This edn.* (*Daniel Cory*);   39. chew'd] *Bullen;* shew'd *Q.*
great *Q.*

24. *the port of her*] her mode of life.
26. *underpoised*] undervalued.   26. *uneven*] unjust.
26. *currents*] makes current, or legal tender.
27. *opinion*] mere sense impression.
29. *part*] role.
32. *Burgomasco*] native of Bergamo (? a bumpkin).
36. *forerunning*] that runs in front, like a fox pursued by hounds.
37. *champing*] chewing up.

FELICHE.

The wolf that eats into the breast of princes, that breeds the 45
lethargy and falling sickness in honor, makes Justice look
asquint and blinks the eye of merited reward from viewing
desertful virtue.

ALBERTO.

What's all this periphrasis, ha?

FELICHE.

The substance of a supple-chapp'd flatterer. 50

ALBERTO.

O, doth he play Forobosco the parasite? Good i' faith.
Sirrah, you must seem now as glib and straight in outward
semblance as a lady's busk, though inwardly as cross as a
pair of tailor's legs; having a tongue as nimble as his needle,
with servile patches of glavering flattery to stitch up the 55
bracks of unworthily honor'd.

FOROBOSCO.

I warrant you, I warrant you, you shall see me prove the
very periwig to cover the bald pate of brainless gentility.
Ho, I will so tickle the sense of *bella graziosa madonna* with
the titillation of hyperbolical praise that I'll strike it in the 60
nick, in the very nick, chuck.

FELICHE.

Thou promisest more than I hope any spectator gives faith
of performance. —(*To* Antonio.) But why look you so dusky,
ha?

ANTONIO.

I was never worse fitted since the nativity of my actorship; 65
I shall be hiss'd at, on my life now.

FELICHE.

Why, what must you play?

66. shall] *1633;* shalt *Q.*

---

45. *wolf*] a malignant ulcer.   47. *blinks*] shuts.
50. *supple-chapp'd*] able to use his jaws glibly.   53. *busk*] corset-bone.
53–54. *cross . . . legs*] Tailors sat cross-legged at their work.
55. *glavering*] deceitful.   56. *bracks*] breaks in cloth.
58. *very . . . gentility*] reminiscence of Sylvester's Du Bartas, "periwig
with wool the bald-pate woods."
59. *bella graziosa madonna*] "my lovely and gracious lady."
61. *nick*] the point aimed at (with obscene *double-entendre*).
61. *chuck*] sweetheart.   63. *dusky*] gloomy.

-6-

ANTONIO.

Faith, I know not what, an hermaphrodite, two parts in one;
my true person being Antonio son to the Duke of Genoa,
though for the love of Mellida, Piero's daughter, I take this   70
feigned presence of an Amazon, calling myself Florizel and I
know not what. I a voice to play a lady! I shall ne'er do it.

ALBERTO.

O, an Amazon should have such a voice, virago-like. Not
play two parts in one? away, away; 'tis common fashion.
Nay, if you cannot bear two subtle fronts under one hood,   75
idiot go by, go by, off this world's stage. O time's impurity!

ANTONIO.

Ay, but when use hath taught me action to hit the right
point of a lady's part, I shall grow ignorant, when I must
turn young prince again, how but to truss my hose.

FELICHE.

Tush, never put them off; for women wear the breeches still.   80

MATZAGENTE.

By the bright honor of a Milanoise,
And the resplendent fulgor of this steel,
I will defend the feminine to death,
And ding his spirit to the verge of hell
That dares divulge a lady's prejudice.   85
                Exit [Matzagente, Forobosco, and Balurdo].

FELICHE.

Rampum scrampum, mount tufty Tamburlaine! What
rattling thunderclap breaks from his lips?

ALBERTO.

O, 'tis native to his part. For acting a modern Bragadoch
under the person of Matzagente, the Duke of Milan's son, it

81-85. By . . . prejudice] *As in*   85.1.] *Bullen; Exit Ant. & Al. Q.
Bullen; printed as prose in Q.*

---

75. *bear . . . hood*] be two-faced.
76. *idiot . . . by*] misquotation from Kyd's *The Spanish Tragedy.*
79. *truss my hose*] lace up my breeches.
82. *resplendent fulgor*] bombastic way of saying "shining brightness."
84. *ding*] bang.   85. *prejudice*] weaknesses.
85.1. *Exit . . . Balurdo*] The emendation (see textual notes) depends on
a misreading of "Exit Mat. & al." as "Exit Ant. & Al."
86. *tufty*]? proud, wearing tuftaffeta.   88. *Bragadoch*] boaster.

may seem to suit with good fashion of coherence. 90

PIERO.

But methinks he speaks with a spruce Attic accent of
adulterate Spanish.

ALBERTO.

So 'tis resolv'd. For Milan being half Spanish, half High
Dutch and half Italians, the blood of chiefest houses is
corrupt and mongrel'd; so that you shall see a fellow 95
vainglorious for a Spaniard, gluttonous for a Dutchman,
proud for an Italian, and a fantastic idiot for all. Such a one
conceit this Matzagente.

FELICHE.

But I have a part allotted me which I have neither able
apprehension to conceit nor what I conceit gracious 100
ability to utter.

GALEATZO.

Whoop, in the old cut? Good, show us a draught of thy
spirit.

FELICHE.

'Tis steady, and must seem so impregnably fortress'd with
his own content that no envious thought could ever invade 105
his spirit; never surveying any man so unmeasuredly happy
whom I thought not justly hateful for some true impoverish-
ment; never beholding any favor of Madam Felicity gracing
another, which his well-bounded content persuaded not to
hang in the front of his own fortune; and therefore as far 110
from envying any man as he valued all men infinitely
distant from accomplish'd beatitude. These native adjuncts
appropriate to me the name of Feliche. [*To* Galeatzo.]
But last, good, thy humor. *Exit* Alberto

ANTONIO.

'Tis to be describ'd by signs and tokens. For unless I were 115

91–92. *spruce . . . Spanish*] as neat and pure as Spanish mixed with
Italian.
93–94. *For Milan . . . Italians*] Milan was under the German (High
Dutch) Spanish rule bequeathed by Charles V.
100. *conceit*] understand. 102. *cut*] groove, rut, vein.
111. *as he valued*] as if he valued.
112. *accomplish'd*] achieved.
113. *Feliche*] see "Names of the Actors."

possess'd with a legion of spirits 'tis impossible to be made
perspicuous by any utterance: for sometimes he must take
austere state as for the person of Galeatzo, the son of the
Duke of Florence, and possess his exterior presence with a
formal majesty, keep popularity in distance; and on the   120
sudden fling his honor so prodigally into a common arm that
he may seem to give up his indiscretion to the mercy of
vulgar censure; now as solemn as a traveler and as grave as
a puritan's ruff; with the same breath as slight and scatter'd
in his fashion as-as-as—a-a-anything. Now, as sweet and   125
neat as a barber's casting-bottle; straight, as slovenly as the
yeasty breast of an ale-knight; now lamenting, then chafing,
straight laughing, then—

FELICHE.
What then?

ANTONIO.
Faith, I know not what. 'T'ad been a right part for Proteus   130
or Gew; ho, blind Gew would ha' done't rarely, rarely.

FELICHE.
I fear it is not possible to limn so many persons in so small a
tablet as the compass of our plays afford.

ANTONIO.
Right. Therefore I have heard that those persons, as he and
you, Feliche, that are but slightly drawn in this comedy,   135
should receive more exact accomplishment in a second part;
which, if this obtain gracious acceptance, means to try his
fortune.

FELICHE.
Peace, here comes the Prologue. Clear the stage.   *Exeunt.*

116–117. *'tis . . . utterance*] it cannot be made clear by words.
118. *state*] royal condition.
123–124. *as grave . . . ruff*] i.e., small, neat, unflamboyant.
126. *casting-bottle*] scent bottle.
127. *yeasty breast*] beery breath.
130. *'T'ad*] it had.
130. *Proteus*] Greek sea god, especially adept at changing his shape.
131. *blind Gew*] has been conjectured to be a "blind performing baboon."
134. *he*] i.e., Galeatzo.
136. *more exact accomplishment*] Feliche does not appear in Part 2; but I
assume the same actor played Pandulpho Feliche there.

[Enter] *the* Prologue.

The wreath of pleasure, and delicious sweets,
Begirt the gentle front of this fair troop!
Select and most respected auditors,
For wit's sake do not dream of miracles;
Alas, we shall but falter if you lay   5
The least sad weight of an unused hope
Upon our weakness; only we give up
The worthless present of slight idleness
To your authentic censure. O that our muse
Had those abstruse and sinewy faculties   10
That, with a strain of fresh invention,
She might press out the rarity of art,
The pur'st elixed juice of rich conceit,
In your attentive ears, that, with the lip
Of gracious elocution, we might drink   15
A sound carouse unto your health of wit.
But O, the heathy dryness of her brain,
Foil to your fertile spirits, is asham'd
To breathe her blushing numbers to such ears.
Yet, most ingenious, deign to veil our wants,   20
With sleek acceptance polish these rude scenes,
And if our slightness your large hope beguiles,
Check not with bended brow, but dimpled smiles.

Exit Prologue.

---

1. *wreath*] garland.   1. *sweets*] flowers.
2. *gentle front*] noble forehead.   2. *this fair troop*] i.e., the audience.
6. *least sad*] lightest.   6. *unused*] unaccustomed.
8. *The . . . idleness*] i.e., this present poor affair, the easy production of an idle moment. Cf. Dedication, 7–8.
10. *abstruse*] secret, hidden (in contrast to *sinewy*).
11. *strain*] (1) a stream or flow; (2) a muscular effort.
13. *elixed*] distilled.   13. *conceit*] conception.
14–16. *that . . . wit*] that we might toast the health of your wit with the kind of eloquence which pleases.
18. *Foil*] opposite.   19. *numbers*] verses.
20. *veil our wants*] conceal our insufficiencies.
21. *sleek*] with reference to the "sleekstone," or polishing stone.
23. *Check*] rebuke.

Antonio and Mellida

The cornets sound a battle within. Enter Antonio *disguised like an* Amazon.

ANTONIO.

Heart, wilt not break? And thou, abhorred life,
Wilt thou still breathe in my enraged blood?
Veins, sinews, arteries, why crack ye not,
Burst and divuls'd with anguish of my grief?
Can man by no means creep out of himself   5
And leave the slough of viperous grief behind?
Antonio, hast thou seen a fight at sea,
As horrid as the hideous day of doom,
Betwixt thy father, Duke of Genoa,
And proud Piero, the Venetian Prince,   10
In which the sea hath swoll'n with Genoa's blood
And made spring tides with the warm reeking gore
That gush'd from out our galley's scupper holes,
In which thy father, poor Andrugio,
Lies sunk or, leapt into the arms of chance,   15
Chok'd with the laboring ocean's brackish foam;
Who, even despite Piero's canker'd hate,
Would with an armed hand have seiz'd thy love
And link'd thee to the beauteous Mellida?
Have I outliv'd the death of all these hopes,   20
Have I felt anguish pour'd into my heart,
Burning like balsamum in tender wounds,
And yet dost live? Could not the fretting sea
Have roll'd me up in wrinkles of his brow?
Is death grown coy, or grim confusion nice,   25

---

4. *divuls'd*] torn asunder.
6. *slough*] the cast skin of a snake.
22. *balsamum*] ointment.
25. *nice*] fastidious.

That it will not accompany a wretch,
But I must needs be cast on Venice shore
And try new fortunes with this strange disguise
To purchase my adored Mellida?

The cornets sound a flourish. Cease.

Hark how Piero's triumphs beat the air.   30
O rugged mischief, how thou grat'st my heart!
Take spirit, blood; disguise, be confident;
Make a firm stand; here rests the hope of all:
Lower than hell there is no depth to fall.

The cornets sound a sennet. Enter Feliche *and* Alberto, *Castilio and*
Forobosco, *a page carrying a shield,* Piero *in armor, Catzo and Dildo and*
Balurdo. *All these (saving* Piero) *armed with petronels. Being enter'd, they*
make a stand in divided files.

PIERO.
Victorious Fortune, with triumphant hand,   35
Hurleth my glory 'bout this ball of earth,
Whilst the Venetian Duke is heaved up
On wings of fair success to overlook
The low-cast ruins of his enemies;
To see myself ador'd and Genoa quake,   40
My fate is firmer than mischance can shake.
FELICHE.
Stand! The ground trembleth.
PIERO.
                         Ha! an earthquake!
BALURDO.
O, I smell a sound.
FELICHE.
Piero, stay! for I descry a fume
Creeping from out the bosom of the deep,   45
The breath of darkness, fatal when 'tis whist

---

34. *Lower . . . fall*] cf. Tilley, *Proverbs*, G 464.
34.1. *sennet*] a set of notes used to indicate a ceremonial entry or exit.
34.3. *petronels*] large pistols.
34.4. *divided files*] military order.
46. *whist*] kept quiet.

In greatness' stomach. This same smoke, call'd pride,
Take heed, she'll lift thee to improvidence
And break thy neck from steep security;
She'll make thee grudge to let Jehovah share   50
In thy successful battles; O, she's ominous,
Enticeth princes to devour heaven,
Swallow omnipotence, outstare dread fate,
Subdue eternity in giant thought,
Heaves up their heart with swelling puff'd conceit   55
Till their souls burst with venom'd arrogance.
Beware, Piero, Rome itself hath tried;
Confusion's train blows up this Babel pride.

PIERO.
Pish! *Dimitto superos, summa votorum attigi.*
Alberto, hast thou yielded up our fix'd decree   60
Unto the Genoan ambassador?
Are they content, if that their Duke return,
To send his and his son Antonio's head,
As pledges steep'd in blood, to gain their peace?

ALBERTO.
With most obsequious, sleek-brow'd entertain,   65
They all embrace it as most gracious.

PIERO.
Are proclamations sent through Italy
That whosoever brings Andrugio's head,
Or young Antonio's, shall be guerdoned
With twenty thousand double pistolets   70
And be endeared to Piero's love?

FOROBOSCO.
They are sent every way; sound policy,
Sweet lord.

55. heart] *Bullen;* hurt *Q.*   71. endeared] *1633;* indeened *Q.*

47. *stomach*] (1) digestion; (2) pride.
49. *security*] culpable self-confidence.   52. *devour*] trisyllabic.
58. *train*] (1) fuse of gunpowder; (2) consequence.
58. *Babel*] (1) towering; (2) leading up to (linguistic) confusion.
59. *Dimitto . . . attigi*] "I dismiss the gods; I have achieved the fulfilment
of prayers" (Seneca *Thyestes* 888).
65. *sleek-brow'd entertain*] deferential reception.

-13-

FELICHE (*aside*).

Confusion to these limber sycophants!

No sooner mischief's born in regency   75

But flattery christens it with "policy."

PIERO.

Why then: *O me coelitum excelsissimum!*

The intestine malice and inveterate hate

I always bore to that Andrugio

Glories in triumph o'er his misery;   80

Nor shall that carpet-boy, Antonio,

Match with my daughter, sweet-cheek'd Mellida.

No, the public power makes my faction strong.

FELICHE.

Ill, when public power strength'neth private wrong.

PIERO.

'Tis horselike not for man to know his force.   85

FELICHE.

'Tis godlike for a man to feel remorse.

PIERO.

Pish! I prosecute my family's revenge,

Which I'll pursue with such a burning chase

Till I have dried up all Andrugio's blood.

Weak rage, that with slight pity is withstood.   90

The cornets sound a flourish.

What means that fresh triumphal flourish sound?

ALBERTO.

The prince of Milan, and young Florence heir,

Approach to gratulate your victory.

PIERO.

We'll girt them with an ample waist of love.

---

74. *limber*] pliant.   75. *regenty*] rule, government.

77. *O me . . . excelsissimum*] "I am the highest of the gods" (Seneca *Thyestes* 911).

81. *carpet-boy*] milksop.   83. *faction*] private mischief.

84. *Ill*] it is a bad thing.

85. *horselike*] bestial (paraphrased from Seneca *Octavia* 453).

86. *remorse*] pity.   93. *gratulate*] congratulate.

94. *We'll . . . love*] We'll throw round them an embrace large enough to span even an ample waist.

Conduct them to our presence royally. 95
Let volleys of the great artillery
From off our galleys' banks play prodigal
And sound loud welcome from their bellowing mouths.

Exit Piero *tantum.*

The cornets sound a sennet. Enter above, Mellida, Rossaline *and* Flavia.
Enter below Galeatzo *with attendants;* Piero [*enters,*] *meeteth him,
embraceth; at which the cornets sound a flourish.* Piero *and* Galeatzo *exeunt.
The rest stand still.*

MELLIDA.
What prince was that passed through my father's guard?
FLAVIA.
'Twas Galeatzo, the young Florentine. 100
ROSSALINE.
Troth, one that will besiege thy maidenhead,
Enter the walls, i' faith, sweet Mellida,
If that thy flankers be not cannonproof.
MELLIDA.
O Mary Ambree! good thy judgment, wench,
Thy bright elections clear; what will he prove? 105
ROSSALINE.
H'ath a short finger and a naked chin,
A skipping eye; dare lay my judgment, faith,
His love is glibbery; there's no hold on't, wench.
Give me a husband whose aspect is firm,
A full-cheek'd gallant with a bouncing thigh— 110
O, he is the *paradiso delle madonne contente.*
MELLIDA.
Even such a one was my Antonio.

---

97. *banks*]? gun-decks.
97. *play prodigal*] fire without counting the cost.
98.1. *Piero tantum*] only Piero.
98.2. *above*] on the upper stage.
103. *flankers*] side-forts.
104. *Mary Ambree*] military heroine of the ballads (suggested by the military images, ll. 101–103).
105. *Thy . . . clear*] give reasons for your choice.
108. *glibbery*] slippery.
111. *paradiso . . . contente*] "the paradise of happy women."

The cornets sound a sennet.

ROSSALINE.
By my nine and thirtieth servant, sweet,
Thou art in love. But stand on tiptoes, fair,
Here comes Saint Tristram Tirlery Whiff, i' faith.   115

Enter Matzagente; Piero [*enters,*] *meets him, embraceth; at which the cornets sound a flourish. They two stand, using seeming compliments, whilst the scene passeth above.*

MELLIDA.
Saint Mark, Saint Mark! What kind of thing appears?
ROSSALINE.
For fancy's passion, spit upon him. Fie!
His face is varnish'd; in the name of love,
What country bred that creature?
MELLIDA.
What is he, Flavia?   120
FLAVIA.
The heir of Milan, Signior Matzagent.
ROSSALINE.
Matzagent? Now by my pleasure's hope,
He is made like a tilting-staff, and looks
For all the world like an o'er-roasted pig;
A great tobacco-taker too, that's flat;   125
For his eyes look as if they had been hung
In the smoke of his nose.
MELLIDA.
What husband will he prove, sweet Rossaline?
ROSSALINE.
Avoid him; for he hath a dwindled leg,
A low forehead and a thin coal-black beard,   130

114. tiptoes] *This edn.;* tiptoed *Q.*

---

113. *servant*] sworn lover.
115. *Tirlery*] trifling, trumpery.
115.2–3. *using . . . above*] Piero and Matzagente make complimentary gestures on the lower stage, while the following episode is being spoken on the upper stage.
118. *varnish'd*] i.e., with cosmetics.
123. *tilting-staff*] a wooden spear used in tournaments.

And will be jealous too, believe it, sweet;
For his chin sweats, and h'ath a gander neck,
A thin lip and a little monkey'sh eye.
Precious! What a slender waist he hath!
He looks like a maypole, or a notched stick.   135
He'll snap in two at every little strain.
Give me a husband that will fill mine arms,
Of steady judgment, quick and nimble sense;
Fools relish not a lady's excellence.

Exeunt all on the lower stage; at which the cornets sound a flourish and a peal of shot is given.

MELLIDA.

The triumph's ended; but look, Rossaline,   140
What gloomy soul in strange accouterments
Walks on the pavement.

ROSSALINE.

Good sweet, let's to her, pray thee, Mellida.

MELLIDA.

How covetous thou art of novelties!

ROSSALINE.

Pish! 'tis our nature to desire things   145
That are thought strangers to the common cut.

MELLIDA.

I am exceeding willing, but—

ROSSALINE.

But what? Pray thee, go down; let's see her face.
God send that neither wit nor beauty wants,
Those tempting sweets, affection's adamants.   *Exeunt.* 150

ANTONIO.

Come down; she comes like—O, no simile
Is precious, choice or elegant enough
To illustrate her descent. Leap heart, she comes,
She comes. Smile heaven, and softest southern wind
Kiss her cheek gently with perfumed breath;   155
She comes. Creation's purity, admir'd,
Ador'd, amazing rarity, she comes.

---

140. *triumph*] celebration of victory.
150. *affection's adamants*] Wit and beauty are the magnets to draw affection.

O now, Antonio, press thy spirit forth
In following passion, knit thy senses close,
Heap up thy powers, double all thy man.   160

Enter Mellida, Rossaline, *and* Flavia.

She comes. O how her eyes dart wonder on my heart!
Mount blood, soul, to my lips; taste Hebe's cup;
Stand firm on deck when beauty's close-fight's up.

MELLIDA.
Lady, your strange habit doth beget
Our pregnant thoughts, even great of much desire   165
To be acquaint with your condition.

ROSSALINE.
Good sweet lady, without more ceremonies,
What country claims your birth? and, sweet, your name?

ANTONIO.
In hope your bounty will extend itself
In selfsame nature of fair courtesy,   170
I'll shun all niceness; my name's Florizell,
My country Scythia; I am Amazon,
Cast on this shore by fury of the sea.

ROSSALINE.
Nay, faith, sweet creature, we'll not veil our names.
It pleas'd the font to dip me Rossaline;   175
That lady bears the name of Mellida,
The Duke of Venice' daughter.

ANTONIO.
Madam, I am oblig'd to kiss your hand
By imposition of a now dead man. *To* Mellida, *kissing her hand.*

---

159. *following*] commensurate with its object.
160. *man*] manhood.
162. *Hebe's cup*] heavenly drink.
163. *Stand . . . deck*] i.e., do not retreat.
163. *close-fight*] a strong point erected on deck as a citadel when boarding engagements are expected.
165. *great*] pregnant.
166. *your condition*] i.e., who and whence you are.
169–170. *In . . . courtesy*] I hope that you will be so good as to tell me the same kind of thing about yourselves.
171. *niceness*] modesty.
175. *It . . . me*] i.e., I was christened.

ROSSALINE.

Now, by my troth, I long beyond all thought   180
To know the man; sweet beauty, deign his name.

ANTONIO.

Lady, the circumstance is tedious.

ROSSALINE.

Troth, not a whit. Good fair, let's have it all;
I love not, I, to have a jot left out   ·
If the tale come from a lov'd orator.   185

ANTONIO.

Vouchsafe me then your hush'd observances.
Vehement in pursuit of strange novelties,
After long travel through the Asian main,
I shipp'd my hopeful thoughts for Brittainy,
Longing to view great nature's miracle,   190
The glory of our sex, whose fame doth strike
Remotest ears with adoration.
Sailing some two months with inconstant winds,
We view'd the glistering Venetian forts
To which we made, when, lo, some three leagues off,   195
We might descry a horrid spectacle:
The issue of black fury strew'd the sea
With tattered carcases of splitted ships,
Half-sinking, burning, floating topsy-turvy.
Not far from these sad ruins of fell rage   200
We might behold a creature press the waves;
Senseless he sprawl'd, all notch'd with gaping wounds;
To him we made and, short, we took him up.
The first word that he spake was, "Mellida,"
And then he swooned.

MELLIDA.

                    Ay me!

ANTONIO.

                    Why sigh you, fair?   205

---

182. *circumstance*] the details.
185. *orator*] speaker.
186. *Vouchsafe . . . observances*] keep quiet while I speak.
188. *main*] mainland.   189. *Brittainy*] Britain.
190. *great . . . miracle*] i.e., Queen Elizabeth.

ROSSALINE.

Nothing but little humors; good sweet, on.

ANTONIO.

His wounds being dress'd, and life recovered,
We 'gan discourse; when, lo, the sea grew mad,
His bowels rumbling with wind passion.
Straight swarthy darkness popp'd out Phoebus' eye,   210
And blurr'd the jocund face of bright-cheek'd day,
Whilst crudl'd fogs masked even darkness' brow.
Heaven bade 's good night, and the rocks groan'd
At the intestine uproar of the main.
Now gusty flaws struck up the very heels   215
Of our mainmast, whilst the keen lightning shot
Through the black bowels of the quaking air.
Straight chops a wave, and in his slifter'd paunch
Down falls our ship, and there he breaks his neck,
Which in an instant up was belk'd again.   220
When thus this martyr'd soul began to sigh:
"Give me your hand," quoth he, "now do you grasp
Th' unequal mirror of ragg'd misery;
Is't not a horrid storm? O well-shap'd sweet,
Could your quick eye strike through these gashed wounds 225
You should behold a heart, a heart, fair creature,
Raging more wild than is this frantic sea.
Wolt do me a favor if thou chance survive?
But visit Venice, kiss the precious white
Of my most—nay, all, all epithets are base   230
To attribute to gracious Mellida.
Tell her the spirit of Antonio
Wisheth his last gasp breath'd upon her breast."

ROSSALINE.

Why weeps softhearted Florizell?

---

206. *little humors*] a trifling indisposition.
213. *Heaven . . . night*] We couldn't see the sky.
215. *flaws*] squalls.
215–216. *struck . . . mainmast*] made it somersault.
218. *slifter'd*] cloven.
220. *belk'd*] belched, vomited.
223. *unequal mirror*] unmatchable image.
223. *ragg'd*] rough, wretched.

ANTONIO.

Alas, the flinty rocks groan'd at his plaints.   235
"Tell her," quoth he, "that her obdurate sire
Hath crack'd his bosom"; therewithal he wept
And thus sigh'd on, "The sea is merciful;
Look how it gapes to bury all my grief.
Well, thou shalt have it; thou shalt be his tomb.   240
My faith in my love live; in thee, die woe,
Die unmatch'd anguish, die Antonio."
With that he totter'd from the reeling deck
And down he sunk.

ROSSALINE.

Pleasure's body! What makes my lady weep?   245

MELLIDA.

Nothing, sweet Rossaline, but the air's sharp.
My father's palace, madam, will be proud
To entertain your presence if you'll deign
To make repose within. Ay me!

ANTONIO.

Lady, our fashion is not curious.   250

ROSSALINE.

Faith, all the nobler; 'tis more generous.

MELLIDA.

Shall I then know how fortune fell at last,
What succor came or what strange fate ensued?

ANTONIO.

Most willingly; but this same court is vast
And public to the staring multitude.   255

ROSSALINE.

Sweet lady! Nay, good sweet! Now, by my troth,
We'll be bedfellows; dirt on compliment froth!

                    Exeunt, Rossaline *giving* Antonio *the way.*

236–237. *that . . . bosom*] i.e., that Antonio has been murdered by Piero's
refusal to allow the marriage.
250. *our . . . curious*] Amazons are not fastidious.
251. *generous*] well-bred.
254. *vast*] open, unbounded.
257. *dirt . . . froth*] None of these affected manners here.
257.1. *giving . . . way*] Rossaline stands back to give the other "lady"
the precedence.

[II.i] *Enter* Catzo, *with a capon, eating;* Dildo *following him.*

DILDO.

  Ha, Catzo! your master wants a clean trencher. Do you
  hear? Balurdo calls for your diminutive attendance.

CATZO.

  The belly hath no ears, Dildo.

DILDO.

  Good pug, give me some capon.

CATZO.

  No capon; no, not a bit, ye smooth bully. Capon's no meat   5
  for Dildo; milk, milk, ye glibbery urchin, is food for infants.

DILDO.

  Upon mine honor.

CATZO.

  Your honor! with a pah! 'slid, now every jackanapes loads
  his back with the golden coat of honor; every ass puts on the
  lion's skin and roars his honor; "upon your honor!" By my   10
  lady's pantable, I fear I shall live to hear a vintner's boy cry,
  "Tis rich neat canary, upon my honor."

DILDO.

  My stomach's up.

CATZO.

  I think thou art hungry.

DILDO.

  The match of fury is lighted, fastened to the linstock of rage,   15
  and will presently set fire to the touchhole of intemperance,
  discharging the double culverin of my incensement in the
  face of thy opprobrious speech.

CATZO.

  I'll stop the barrel thus [*gives him food*]; good Dildo, set not
  fire to the touchhole.   20

DILDO.

  My rage is stopp'd, and I will eat to the health of the fool
  thy master, Castilio.

---

3. *belly . . . ears*] proverbial; Tilley, B 286.   6. *glibbery*] slippery.
9–10. *every ass . . . skin*] reference to the fable of the ass and the lion-skin.
11. *pantable*] slipper.   13. *stomach*] (1) anger; (2) hunger.
15. *linstock*] a staff to hold the gunner's lighted match.
17. *culverin*] cannon.

CATZO.

And I will suck the juice of the capon to the health of the
idiot thy master, Balurdo.

DILDO.

Faith, our masters are like a case of rapiers sheathed in one   25
scabbard of folly.

CATZO.

Right Dutch blades. But was't not rare sport at the sea-
battle, whilst rounce-robble-hobble roar'd from the ship
sides, to view our masters pluck their plumes and drop their
feathers for fear of being men of mark.   30

DILDO.

"'Slud," cried Signior Balurdo, "O for Don Besicleer's
armor, in the Mirror of Knighthood! What coil's here? O
for an armor, cannonproof! O, more cable, more featherbeds, more featherbeds, more cable!" till he had as much as
my cable hatband to fence him.   35

Enter Flavia *in haste, with a rebato.*

CATZO.

Buxom Flavia, can you sing? song, song!

FLAVIA.

My sweet Dildo, I am not for you at this time. Madam
Rossaline stays for a fresh ruff to appear in the presence.
Sweet, away!

DILDO.

'Twill not be so put off, delicate, delicious, spark-eyed,   40

---

25. *case*] pair.
27. *Dutch blades*] presumably derogatory.
28. *rounce-robble-hobble*] the noise of the cannon.
29–30. *pluck . . . feathers*] (1) take off their be-plumed officers' helmets;
(2) lose their pride.
30. *men of mark*] (1) important persons; (2) targets for the guns.
32. *Mirror of Knighthood*] Spanish romance, much mocked at by the wits;
the hero is called *Rosicler*, but Balurdo's error may be intended.
32. *coil*] fuss.
33–34. *more cable . . . cable*] Featherbeds were roped on doors, etc., to
absorb gunshot. Coils of rope seem to have been used for the same purpose.
35. *cable hatband*] a twisted cord worn round the hat; a mark of gentility.
35.1. *rebato*] a stiff collar used to support a ruff.
38. *presence*] the chamber where the sovereign held court.

sleek-skinn'd, slender-waisted, clean-legg'd, rarely shap'd—

FLAVIA.

Who? I'll be at all your service another season. Nay, faith, there's reason in all things.

DILDO.

Would I were reason, then, that I might be in all things.

CATZO.

The brief and the semiquaver is, we must have the descant 45
you made upon our names, ere you depart.

FLAVIA.

Faith, the song will seem to come off hardly.

CATZO.

Troth, not a whit; if you seem to come off quickly.

FLAVIA.

Pert Catzo! Knock it lustily then.

Cantant.

Enter Forobosco *with two torches,* Castilio *singing fantastically,* Rossaline *running a coranto pace, and* Balurdo; Feliche *following, wondering at them all.*

FOROBOSCO.

Make place, gentlemen; pages, hold torches; the prince 50
approacheth the presence.

DILDO.

What squeaking cart wheel have we here? ha? "Make place, gentlemen; pages, hold torches; the prince approacheth the presence."

ROSSALINE.

Foh, what a strong scent's here! somebody useth to wear 55
socks.

BALURDO.

By this fair candlelight 'tis not my feet. I never wore socks since I suck'd pap.

---

45. *brief . . . semiquaver*] the long and the short (pun on *breve*).
46. *our names*] see "The Names of the Actors."
49. *Knock it*] strike up.
49.1. *Cantant*] "They sing."
49.3. *running a coranto pace*] using the steps of the *coranto* (a lively running dance).

ROSSALINE.

Savorly put off.

CASTILIO.

Ha, her wit stings, blisters, galls off the skin with the tart 60
acrimony of her sharp quickness. By sweetness, she is the
very Pallas that flew out of Jupiter's brainpan. Delicious
creature, vouchsafe me your service; by the purity of bounty
I shall be proud of such bondage.

ROSSALINE.

I vouchsafe it; be my slave. Signior Balurdo, wilt thou be my 65
servant too?

BALURDO.

O God, forsooth, in very good earnest, la, you would make
me as a man should say—as a man should say.

FELICHE.

'Slud, sweet beauty, will you deign him your service?

ROSSALINE.

O, your fool is your only servant. But good Feliche, why art 70
thou so sad? A penny for thy thought, man.

FELICHE.

I sell not my thought so cheap; I value my meditation at a
higher rate.

BALURDO.

In good sober sadness, sweet mistress, you should have had
my thought for a penny; by this crimson satin that cost 75
eleven shillings, thirteen pence, three pence halfpenny a
yard, that you should, la.

ROSSALINE.

What was thy thought, good servant?

BALURDO.

Marry, forsooth, how many strike of pease would feed a hog
fat against Christ-tide. 80

---

59. *Savorly*] (1) wisely; (2) stinkingly.
62. *Pallas . . . brainpan*] Pallas (or *wit*) grew in the skull of her father
Jupiter.
63. *service*] permission to serve.
63. *bounty*] virtue (with a jingle on *bondage*).
66. *servant*] bound lover.
74. *sadness*] seriousness.
79. *strike*] bushels.   80. *Christ-tide*] Christmas.

ROSSALINE.

Poh! [*She spits.*] Servant, rub out my rheum; it soils the
presence.

CASTILIO.

By my wealthiest thought, you grace my shoe with an unmeasured honor; I will preserve the sole of it as a most
sacred relic, for this service.   85

ROSSALINE.

I'll spit in thy mouth, and thou wilt, to grace thee.

FELICHE.

O that the stomach of this queasy age
Digests or brooks such raw unseasoned gobs
And vomits not them forth! O slavish sots!
"Servant," quoth you? Foh! If a dog should crave   90
And beg her service, he should have it straight.
She'd give him favors too, to lick her feet,
Or fetch her fan, or some such drudgery—
A good dog's office, which these amorists
Triumph of. 'Tis rare. Well, give her more ass,   95
More sot, as long as dropping of her nose
Is sworn rich pearl by such low slaves as those.

ROSSALINE.

Flavia, attend me to attire me.   *Exit* Rossaline *and* Flavia.

BALURDO.

In sad good earnest, sir, you have touch'd the very bare of
naked truth; my silk stocking hath a good gloss and I thank 100
my planets my leg is not altogether unpropitiously shap'd.
There's a word: "unpropitiously." I think I shall speak
"unpropitiously" as well as any courtier in Italy.

FOROBOSCO.

So help me your sweet bounty, you have the most graceful
presence, applausive elocuty, amazing volubility, polish'd 105
adornation, delicious affability—

FELICHE.

Whop! Fut, how he tickles yon trout under the gills! You
shall see him take him by and by with groping flattery.

---

96. *as long*] so long.
105. *applausive elocuty*] style worthy of applause.

FOROBOSCO.

—that ever ravish'd the ear of wonder. By your sweet self,
than whom I know not a more exquisite, illustrate, accom-   110
plished, pure, respected, ador'd, observed, precious, real,
magnanimous, bounteous—if you have an idle rich cast
jerkin or so, it shall not be cast away, if—Ha! here's a
forehead, an eye, a head, a hair that would make a—or if
you have any spare pair of silver spurs, I'll do you as much   115
right in all kind offices—

FELICHE.

—of a kind parasite.

FOROBOSCO.

—as any of my mean fortunes shall be able to.

BALURDO.

As I am true Christian now, thou hast won the spurs.

FELICHE.

—for flattery.   120
O how I hate that same Egyptian louse,
A rotten maggot that lives by stinking filth
Of tainted spirits. Vengeance to such dogs
That sprout by gnawing senseless carrion!

Enter Alberto.

ALBERTO.

Gallants, saw you my mistress, the Lady Rossaline?   125

FOROBOSCO.

My mistress, the Lady Rossaline, left the presence even now.

CASTILIO.

My mistress, the Lady Rossaline, withdrew her gracious
aspect even now.

BALURDO.

My mistress, the Lady Rossaline, withdrew her gracious
aspect even now.   130

FELICHE.

Well said, echo.

---

110. *illustrate*] illustrious.   111. *real*] royal.
112–113. *idle . . . jerkin*] a rich secondhand jerkin that is not much cared
about.
121. *Egyptian louse*] i.e., as in the Mosaic plague (Exodus 8:16 ff.).
123. *to*] on.

ALBERTO.

My mistress, and his mistress, and your mistress, and the
dog's mistress—precious dear heaven, that Alberto lives to
have such rivals!
'Slid, I have been searching every private room,   135
Corner and secret angle of the court,
And yet, and yet, and yet she lives conceal'd.
Good sweet Feliche, tell me how to find
My bright-fac'd mistress out.

FELICHE.

Why man, cry out for lanthorn and candlelight. For 'tis your 140
only way to find your bright flaming wench, with your light
burning torch; for most commonly these light creatures live
in darkness.

ALBERTO.

Away, you heretic; you'll be burnt for—

FELICHE.

Go, you amorous hound; follow the scent of your mistress' 145
shoe. Away.   [*Exit* Alberto.]

FOROBOSCO.

Make a fair presence; boys, advance your lights; the
Princess makes approach.

BALURDO.

And please the gods, now in very good deed, la, you shall
see me tickle the measures for the heavens. Do my hangers 150
show?

Enter Piero, Antonio, Mellida, Rossaline, Galeatzo, Matzagente,
Alberto, *and* Flavia. *As they enter,* Feliche *and* Castilio *make a rank for
the* Duke *to pass through.* Forobosco *ushers the* Duke *to his state; then
whilst* Piero *speaketh his first speech,* Mellida *is taken by* Galeatzo *and*
Matzagente *to dance, they supporting her;* Rossaline *in like manner by*
Alberto *and* Balurdo; Flavia *by* Feliche *and* Castilio.

---

140. *lanthorn and candlelight*] the call of the bellman.
150. *tickle . . . heavens*] leap heaven-high in the dance.
150. *hangers*] the straps by which the sword (or dagger) was suspended.
151.3. *state*] throne.
151.5. *they supporting her*] one on either side, like heraldic "supporters."

PIERO.

    Beauteous Amazon, sit, and seat your thoughts
    In the reposure of most soft content.
    Sound music there! Nay daughter, clear your eyes
    From these dull fogs of misty discontent.   155
    Look sprightly, girl. What! Though Antonio's drown'd,
    That peevish dotard on thy excellence,
    That hated issue of Andrugio,
    Yet may'st thou triumph in my victories;
    Since, lo, the highborn bloods of Italy   160
    Sue for thy seat of love. Let music sound!
    Beauty and youth run descant on love's ground.
                           [*Music sounds, for dancing.*]

MATZAGENTE.

    Lady, erect your gracious symmetry;
    Shine in the sphere of sweet affection
    Your eye, as heavy as the heart of night.   165

MELLIDA.

    My thoughts are as black as your beard, my fortunes as
    ill-proportioned as your legs, and all the powers of my mind
    as leaden as your wit and as dusty as your face is swarthy.

GALEATZO.

    Faith, sweet, I'll lay thee on the lips for that jest.

MELLIDA.

    I pray thee intrude not on a dead man's right.   170

GALEATZO.

    No; but the living's just possession,
    Thy lips and love are mine.

MELLIDA.

    You ne'er took seisin on them yet; forbear!
    There's not a vacant corner of my heart,

161. Let . . . sound] *Bullen;* printed
as S.D. in Q.

___

    162. *run . . . ground*] make sprightly melodies above the plainsong
bass-line of love.
    163. *erect . . . symmetry*] i.e., stand up (to dance).
    164–165. *Shine . . . night*] Let your eye, which is now as gloomy as night,
shine in the area proper to love.
    173. *seisin*] legal possession.

But all is fill'd with dead Antonio's loss.   175
Then urge no more; O, leave to love at all;
'Tis less disgraceful not to mount than fall.

MATZAGENTE.

Bright and refulgent lady, deign your ear;
You see this blade; had it a courtly lip
It would divulge my valor, plead my love,   180
Justle that skipping feeble amorist
Out of your love's seat; I am Matzagent.

GALEATZO.

Hark thee; I pray thee taint not thy sweet ear
With that sot's gabble; by thy beauteous cheek,
He is the flagging'st bulrush that e'er droop'd   185
With each slight mist of rain. But with pleas'd eye
Smile on my courtship.

MELLIDA.

What said you, sir? Alas my thought was fix'd
Upon another object. Good, forbear;
I shall but weep. Ay me, what boots a tear!   190
Come, come, let's dance. O music, thou distill'st
More sweetness in us than this jarring world;
Both time and measure from thy strains do breathe,
Whilst from the channel of this dirt doth flow
Nothing but timeless grief, unmeasured woe.   195

ANTONIO.

O how impatience cramps my cracked veins,
And cruddles thick my blood with boiling rage.
O eyes, why leap you not like thunderbolts
Or cannon bullets in my rivals' face?
Ohimè infelice misero, o lamentevol fato.   [*Falls on the ground.*] 200

ALBERTO.

What means the lady fall upon the ground?

---

178. *refulgent*] glittering.
190. *boots*] matters.
193. *time and measure*] the duration of the note and the rhythm by which
these durations are organized.
194. *channel*] the open sewer of Elizabethan streets.
194. *this dirt*] the vile earth.
197. *cruddles*] curdles.
200. *Ohimè . . . fato*] "Alas, unfortunate, wretched, lamentable fate."

ROSSALINE.

Belike the falling sickness.

ANTONIO.

I cannot brook this sight; my thoughts grow wild;
Here lies a wretch on whom heaven never smil'd.

ROSSALINE.

What, servant, ne'er a word, and I here, man?   205
I would shoot some speech forth to strike the time
With pleasing touch of amorous compliment.
Say, sweet, what keeps thy mind? what think'st thou on?

ALBERTO.

Nothing.

ROSSALINE.

What's that nothing?   210

ALBERTO.

A woman's constancy.

ROSSALINE.

Good, why, would'st thou have us sluts, and never shift the
vesture of our thoughts? Away for shame!

ALBERTO.

O no, th'art too constant to afflict my heart,
Too too firm fixed in unmoved scorn.   215

ROSSALINE.

Pish, pish. I fixed in unmoved scorn?
Why, I'll love thee tonight.

ALBERTO.

But whom tomorrow?

ROSSALINE.

Faith, as the toy puts me in the head.

BALURDO.

And pleased the marble heavens, now would I might be the 220
toy, to put you in the head kindly to conceit my—my—my—
pray you give m' an epithet for love.

FELICHE.

"Roaring," "roaring."

222. m' an] *This edn.;* in an *Q.*

---

202. *the falling sickness*] epilepsy (with the usual *double-entendre* on female
liability to fall).

214. *constant to afflict*] consistent in afflicting.   219. *toy*] whim.

BALURDO.

O love, thou hast murder'd me, made me a shadow, and
you hear not Balurdo, but Balurdo's ghost.   225

ROSSALINE.

Can a ghost speak?

BALURDO.

Scurvily, as I do.

ROSSALINE.

And walk?

BALURDO.

After their fashion.

ROSSALINE.

And eat apples?   230

BALURDO.

In a sort; in their garb.

FELICHE.

Pray thee, Flavia, be my mistress.

FLAVIA.

Your reason, good Feliche?

FELICHE.

Faith, I have nineteen mistresses already, and I not much
disdain that thou should'st make up the full score.   235

FLAVIA.

O, I hear you make commonplaces of your mistresses, to
perform the office of memory by. Pray you, in ancient times
were not those satin hose? In good faith, now they are new
dyed, pink'd and scoured, they show as well as if they were
new. What, mute, Balurdo?   240

FELICHE.

Ay, in faith; and 'twere not for printing and painting, my
breech and your face would be out of reparation.

BALURDO.

Ay, in faith, and 'twere not for printing and painting, my

224. S.P. BALURDO.] *Bullen; speech*   243. in] *Bullen; an Q.*
continued to Feliche in Q.   243. painting] *1633;* pointing *Q.*

224–229] From Erasmus' Colloquies ("Proci et Puellae").
  236. *commonplaces*] chapter headings, used to memorize quotations, ideas.
  241–242. *and 'twere . . . reparation*] The same joke appears in the *Merry
Jests of George Peele,* where "printing" seems to mean "dyeing."

breech and your face would be out of reparation.

FELICHE.

Good again, echo.   245

FLAVIA.

Thou art, by nature, too foul to be affected.

FELICHE.

And thou, by art, too fair to be beloved.

By wit's life, most spark spirit's but hard chance.

La ty dine.

PIERO.

Gallants, the night grows old, and downy sleep   250

Courts us to entertain his company;

Our tired limbs, bruis'd in the morning fight,

Entreat soft rest and gentle hush'd repose.

Fill out Greek wines; prepare fresh cresset-light;

We'll have a banquet, princes, then good night.   255

The cornets sound a sennet and the Duke *goes out in state. As they are going out,* Antonio *stays* Mellida; *the rest exeunt.*

ANTONIO.

What means these scatter'd looks? why tremble you?

Why quake your thoughts in your distracted eyes?

Collect your spirits, madam. What do you see?

Dost not behold a ghost?

Look, look where he stalks, wrapp'd up in clouds of grief, 260

Darting his soul upon thy wondering eyes.

Look, he comes towards thee; see, he stretcheth out

His wretched arms to gird thy loved waist

With a most wish'd embrace. See'st him not yet?

Nor yet? Ha, Mellida; thou well may'st err;   265

For look, he walks not like Antonio,

Like that Antonio that this morning shone

In glistering habiliments of arms

---

246. *be affected*] i.e., be enrolled as a lover.   247. *art*] cosmetics.

248. *By . . . chance*] I swear, by the life of wit, that it is a hard fortune to woo a lady of flashing spirit.

249. *La ty dine*] not understood.

254. *cresset-light*] oil lamp.

255. *banquet*] a repast of fruit and wine.

    To seize his love, spite of her father's spite;
    But like himself, wretched and miserable,   270
    Banish'd, forlorn, despairing, struck quite through
    With sinking grief, roll'd up in sevenfold doubles
    Of plagues, unvanquishable. Hark, he speaks to thee.

MELLIDA.
    Alas, I cannot hear nor see him.

ANTONIO.
    Why? All this night about the room he stalk'd   275
    And groan'd and howl'd with raging passion
    To view his love (lifeblood of all his hopes,
    Crown of his fortunes) clipp'd by strangers' arms.
    Look but behind thee.

MELLIDA.
    O Antonio, my lord, my love, my—   280

ANTONIO.
    Leave passion, sweet; for time, place, air and earth
    Are all our foes. Fear and be jealous. Fair,
    Let's fly.

MELLIDA.
    Dear heart, ha, whither?

ANTONIO.
    O, 'tis no matter whither, but let's fly.   285
    Ha! now I think on't, I have ne'er a home,
    No father, friend, no country to embrace
    These wretched limbs. The world, the all that is,
    Is all my foe; a prince not worth a doit!
    Only my head is hoised to high rate,   290
    Worth twenty thousand double pistolets
    To him that can but strike it from these shoulders.
    But come, sweet creature, thou shalt be my home,
    My father, country, riches and my friend,
    My all, my soul; and thou and I will live—   295
    Let's think like what—and thou and I will live

273. unvanquishable] *Bullen;* van-
quishable *Q.*

---

272. *sinking*] capable of causing to sink.
272. *doubles*] ? folded pieces of cloth.   278. *clipp'd*] embraced.
289. *doit*] coin of small value.   290. *hoised*] raised.

Like unmatch'd mirrors of calamity.
The jealous ear of night eavedrops our talk;
Hold thee; there's a jewel; and look thee, there's a note
That will direct thee when, where, how to fly;   300
Bid me adieu.

MELLIDA.   Farewell, bleak misery.

ANTONIO.
Stay, sweet, let's kiss before you go.

MELLIDA.
Farewell, dear soul.

ANTONIO.
                    Farewell, my life, my heart.   [*Exeunt.*]

[III.i]
Enter Andrugio *in armor,* Lucio *with a shepherd gown in his hand, and a*
page.

ANDRUGIO.
Is not yon gleam the shuddering morn, that flakes
With silver tincture the east verge of heaven?

LUCIO.
I think it is, so please your excellence.

ANDRUGIO.
Away! I have no excellence to please.
Pray thee observe the custom of the world   5
That only flatters greatness, states exalts.
"And please my excellence!" O, Lucio,
Thou hast been ever held respected, dear,
Even precious to Andrugio's inmost love;
Good, flatter not. Nay, if thou giv'st not faith   10
That I am wretched, O read that, read that.

LUCIO [*reads*].
Piero Sforza to the Italian princes, fortune:
Excellent, the just overthrow Andrugio took in the Venetian Gulf

---

297. *unmatch'd mirrors*] unequaled examples.
[III.i]
    0.1. *a shepherd gown*] This he hopes to give to Andrugio to disguise him.
    6. *states*] sovereigns.
    13. *Excellent*] Your Excellencies.

hath so assured the Genoese of the injustice of his cause and the
hatefulness of his person, that they have banish'd him and all his   15
family; and for confirmation of their peace with us have vowed, that
if he or his son can be attached, to send us both their heads. We
therefore by force of our united league forbid you to harbor him or his
blood; but if you apprehend his person we entreat you to send him
or his head to us. For we vow by the honor of our blood to recompense   20
any man that bringeth his head with twenty thousand double
pistolets, and the endearing to our choicest love.

From Venice: Piero Sforza.

ANDRUGIO.

My thoughts are fix'd in contemplation
Why this huge earth, this monstrous animal   25
That eats her children, should not have eyes and ears.
Philosophy maintains that Nature's wise
And forms no useless or unperfect thing.
Did Nature make the earth, or the earth Nature?
For earthly dirt makes all things, makes the man,   30
Molds me up honor; and like a cunning Dutchman
Paints me a puppet even with seeming breath
And gives a sot appearance of a soul.
Go to, go to; thou liest, Philosophy!
Nature forms things unperfect, useless, vain.   35
Why made she not the earth with eyes and ears,
That she might see desert and hear men's plaints?
That when a soul is splitted, sunk with grief,
He might fall thus upon the breast of earth   [*Falls on the ground.*]
And in her ear halloo his misery,   40
Exclaiming thus: "O thou all-bearing earth
Which men do gape for, till thou cramm'st their mouths
And chok'st their throats with dust: O chaune thy breast
And let me sink into thee! Look who knocks;
Andrugio calls. But O, she's deaf and blind;   45
A wretch but lean relief on earth can find.

14. *injustice*] Bullen; *justice Q*.

---

31. *Molds . . . honor*] creates the possessor of honor.
31. *cunning Dutchman*] skillful painter from Holland or Germany.
43. *chaune*] split.

LUCIO.

> Sweet lord, abandon passion, and disarm.
> Since by the fortune of the tumbling sea
> We are roll'd up upon the Venice marsh
> Let's clip all fortune, lest more lowering fate—   50

ANDRUGIO.

> More lowering fate! O Lucio, choke that breath.
> Now I defy chance. Fortune's brow hath frown'd
> Even to the utmost wrinkle it can bend;
> Her venom's spit. Alas, what country rests,
> What son, what comfort, that she can deprive?   55
> Triumphs not Venice in my overthrow?
> Gapes not my native country for my blood?
> Lies not my son tomb'd in the swelling main?
> And yet, more lowering fate? There's nothing left
> Unto Andrugio, but Andrugio;   60
> And that nor mischief, force, distress, nor hell can take.
> Fortune my fortunes, not my mind shall shake.

LUCIO.

> Spoke like yourself; but give me leave, my lord,
> To wish your safety. If you are but seen,
> Your arms display you; therefore put them off   65
> And take—

ANDRUGIO.

> Would'st thou have me go unarm'd among my foes,
> Being besieg'd by passion, entering lists
> To combat with despair and mighty grief,
> My soul beleaguer'd with the crushing strength   70
> Of sharp impatience? Ha, Lucio, go unarm'd?
> Come soul, resume the valor of thy birth;
> Myself myself, will dare all opposites.

63. Spoke] *Bullen;* speake *Q.*

---

50. *clip*] embrace.   54. *rests*] remains.
62. *Fortune . . . shake*] "Fortune may affect my status but not my resolution" (translation of Seneca *Medea* 176).
65. *Your arms display you*] The heraldry on your armor tells who you are.
68. *lists*] the tournament ground.
72. *of thy birth*] that is thy birthright.
73. *Myself myself*] my self being restored to its true condition; cf. l. 113 below.

I'll muster forces, an unvanquish'd power;
Cornets of horse shall press th' ungrateful earth;   75
This hollow-wombed mass shall inly groan
And murmur to sustain the weight of arms;
Ghastly Amazement with upstarted hair
Shall hurry on before and usher us,
Whilst trumpets clamor with a sound of death.   80

LUCIO.

Peace, good my lord; your speech is all too light.
Alas, survey your fortunes, look what's left
Of all your forces and your utmost hopes:
A weak old man, a page, and your poor self.

ANDRUGIO.

Andrugio lives, and a fair cause of arms;   85
Why, that's an army all invincible.
He who hath that hath a battalion royal,
Armor of proof, huge troops of barbed steeds,
Main squares of pikes, millions of harquebus.
O, a fair cause stands firm and will abide;   90
Legions of angels fight upon her side.

LUCIO.

Then, noble spirit, slide in strange disguise
Unto some gracious prince and sojourn there
Till time and fortune give revenge firm means.

ANDRUGIO.

No, I'll not trust the honor of a man.   95
Gold is grown great and makes Perfidiousness
A common waiter in most princes' courts.
He's in the checkle-roll; I'll not trust my blood.
I know none breathing but will cog a die

97. waiter] *1633;* water *Q.*

---

75. *Cornets*] companies of cavalry.
84. *A weak old man*] i.e., Lucio.
85. *a fair . . . arms*] a good reason for fighting.
87. *battalion royal*] ? a large body of soldiers, or a royal bodyguard.
88. *barbed*] wearing horse-armor.
89. *harquebus*] primitive muskets.   92. *slide*] slip away.
97. *waiter*] an attendant; a spy (old form *water*).
98. *checkle-roll*] pun on (1) checker-roll (a list of servants); (2) shekel-roll.
98. *my blood*] my relatives.   99. *cog a die*] cheat at dice.

For twenty thousand double pistolets.   100
How goes the time?
LUCIO.   I saw no sun today.
ANDRUGIO.
No sun will shine where poor Andrugio breathes.
My soul grows heavy; boy, let's have a song.
We'll sing yet, faith, even despite of fate.

Cantant.

ANDRUGIO.
'Tis a good boy; and, by my troth, well sung.   105
O, and thou felt'st my grief, I warrant thee,
Thou would'st have struck division to the height,
And made the life of music breathe. Hold, boy. Why so?
                    [*Boy weeps.*]
For God's sake call me not Andrugio,
That I may soon forget what I have been.   110
For heaven's name, name not Antonio,
That I may not remember he was mine.
Well, ere yon sun set I'll show myself myself,
Worthy my blood. I was a duke; that's all.
No matter whither but from whence we fall.   *Exeunt.* 115

[III.ii]   *Enter* Feliche *walking unbrac'd.*

FELICHE.
Castilio? Alberto? Balurdo? None up?
Forobosco? Flattery, nor thou up yet?
Then there's no courtier stirring; that's firm truth.
I cannot sleep; Feliche seldom rests
In these court lodgings. I have walk'd all night   5
To see if the nocturnal court delights
Could force me envy their felicity;
And by plain truth—I will confess plain truth—

104.1. *Cantant*] "They sing."
107. *struck . . . height*] produced the most exalted kind of music.
115. *No . . . fall*] i.e., it is the achievement of greatness that matters, not
the misery that may be its consequence (from Seneca *Thyestes* 925–926).
[III.ii]
0.1. *unbrac'd*] with his clothes loosened.

I envy nothing but the traverse light.
O, had it eyes and ears and tongues, it might   10
See sport, hear speech of most strange surquedries.
O, if that candlelight were made a poet,
He would prove a rare firking satirist
And draw the core forth of imposthum'd sin.
Well, I thank heaven yet that my content   15
Can envy nothing but poor candlelight.
As for the other glistering copper spangs
That glisten in the tyer of the court,
Praise God I either hate or pity them.
Well, here I'll sleep till that the scene of up   20
Is past at court. [*Lies down.*] O calm, hush'd, rich content,
Is there a being blessedness without thee?
How soft thou down'st the couch where thou dost rest,
Nectar to life, thou sweet ambrosian feast.

Enter Castilio *and his page* [Catzo]; Castilio *with a casting bottle of sweet water in his hand, sprinkling himself.*

CASTILIO.
Am not I a most sweet youth now?   25
CATZO.
Yes, when your throat's perfum'd your very words
Do smell of ambergris. O stay sir, stay!
Sprinkle some sweet water to your shoes' heels,
That your mistress may swear you have a sweet foot.
CASTILIO.
Good, very good, very passing, passing good.   30
FELICHE.
Fut, what treble minikin squeaks there, ha? "Good, very
good, very, very good!"

---

9. *traverse*] partition.
11. *surquedries*] arrogancies, excesses.
13. *firking*] whipping.
14. *imposthum'd*] boil-like, erupting.
17. *copper spangs*] spangles of pretended gold.
18. *tyer*] attire.   20. *the scene of up*] the levee.
22. *being blessedness*] blessedness in existence.
27. *ambergris*] whale secretion used in perfume manufacture.
31. *minikin*] diminutive person.

CASTILIO.

I will warble to the delicious concave of my mistress' ear,
and strike her thoughts with the pleasing touch of my voice.

Cantant.

CASTILIO.

Feliche, health, fortune, mirth and wine—   35

FELICHE.

To thee my love divine.

CASTILIO.

I drink to thee, sweeting.

FELICHE.

Plague on thee for an ass.

CASTILIO.

Now thou hast seen the court, by the perfection of it dost
not envy it?   40

FELICHE.

I wonder it doth not envy me.
Why man, I have been borne upon the spirit's wings,
The soul's swift Pegasus, the fantasy;
And from the height of contemplation
Have view'd the feeble joints men totter on.   45
I envy none, but hate or pity all;
For when I view with an intentive thought
That creature fair, but proud; him rich, but sot;
Th' other witty, but unmeasured arrogant;
Him great, yet boundless in ambition;   50
Him highborn, but of base life; t'other fear'd;
Yet feared fears, and fears most to be most loved;
Him wise, but made a fool for public use;
Th' other learned, but self-opinionate—
When I discourse all these, and see myself   55
Nor fair nor rich nor witty, great, nor fear'd,
Yet amply suited with all full content,
Lord, how I clap my hands and smooth my brow,

---

47. *intentive*] attentive, intensely applied.
52. *feared fears*] the man who frightens others, fears others (from Seneca
Oedipus 705–706).
55. *discourse*] run over.

Rubbing my quiet bosom, tossing up
A grateful spirit to omnipotence.   60

CASTILIO.

Ha, ha! But if thou knew'st my happiness
Thou wouldst even grate away thy soul to dust
In envy of my sweet beatitude.
I cannot sleep for kisses; I cannot rest
For ladies' letters that importune me   65
With such unused vehemence of love
Straight to solicit them, that—

FELICHE.

Confusion seize me, but I think thou liest.
Why should I not be sought to then as well?
Fut! methinks I am as like a man.   70
Troth! I have a good head of hair, a cheek
Not as yet wan'd, a leg, faith, in the full.
I ha' not a red beard, take not tobacco much,
And 'slid, for other parts of manliness—

CASTILIO.

Pew, waw; you ne'er accourted them in pomp,   75
Put your good parts in presence graciously.
Ha, and you had, why they would ha' come off, sprung
To your arms; and su'd and pray'd and vow'd
And opened all their sweetness to your love.

FELICHE.

There are a number of such things as thou   80
Have often urg'd me to such loose belief;
But 'slid, you all do lie, you all do lie.
I have put on good clothes and smugg'd my face,
Struck a fair wench with a smart-speaking eye,
Courted in all sorts, blunt and passionate,   85
Had opportunity, put them to the "ah";
And by this light, I find them wondrous chaste,
Impregnable—perchance a kiss or so;
But for the rest, O most inexorable.

80. thou] *Bullen;* then *Q*.

---

66. *unused*] unprecedented.
73. *red beard*] like Marston himself.
83. *smugg'd*] smoothed.

CASTILIO.

Nay then, i' faith, pray thee look here.   90

        Shows him the superscription of a seeming letter.

FELICHE [*reads*].

"*To her most esteemed, lov'd and generous servant, Signior Castilio
Balthazar.*"

Pray thee, from whom comes this? Faith, I must see.
[*Reads.*] "*From her that is devoted to thee in most private sweets of
love, Rossaline.*"   95

Nay, God's my comfort, I must see the rest;
I must, sans ceremony, faith, I must.

        Feliche *takes away the letter by force.*

CASTILIO.

O, you spoil my ruff, unset my hair; good, away!

FELICHE [*reads*].

"*Item, for straight canvas, thirteen pence halfpenny; item, for an
ell and a half of taffeta to cover your old canvas doublet, fourteen* 100
shillings and three pence." 'Slight, this is a tailor's bill.

CASTILIO.

In sooth, it is the outside of her letter, on which I took the
copy of a tailor's bill.

CATZO.

But 'tis not cross'd, I am sure of that. Lord have mercy on
him, his credit hath given up the last gasp. Faith, I'll leave 105
him; for he looks as melancholy as a wench the first night
she—   *Exit.*

FELICHE.

Honest musk-cod, 'twill not be so stitched together; take
that, and that [*hits him with letter*], and belie no lady's love;
swear no more by Jesu, this madam, that lady; hence, go; 110
forswear the presence; travel three years, to bury this
bastinado. Avoid, puff-paste, avoid!

CASTILIO.

And tell not my lady mother? Well, as I am true gentleman,
if she had not will'd me on her blessing not to spoil my face,
if I could not find in my heart to fight, would I might ne'er 115

---

101. this is] *1633;* this *Q.*   104. S.P. CATZO.] *This edn.; Dil. Q.*

---

104. *cross'd*] written across.   108. *musk-cod*] scent-pod.
112. *bastinado*] beating.   112. *puff-paste*] insubstantial object.

eat a potato pie more.   [*Exit.*]

Enter Balurdo, *backward,* Dildo *following him with a looking glass in one hand and a candle in the other hand,* Flavia *following him backward with a looking glass in one hand and a candle in the other,* Rossaline *following her.* Balurdo *and* Rossaline *stand setting of faces; and so the scene begins.*

FELICHE.

More fools, more rare fools! O, for time and place long enough and large enough to act these fools! Here might be made a rare scene of folly, if the plot could bear it.

BALURDO.

By the sugar-candy sky, hold up the glass higher, that I may   120
see to swear in fashion. O, one loofe more would ha' made
them shine; God's neaks, they would have shone like my
mistress' brow. Even so the Duke frowns, for all this Curson
world. O that girn kills, it kills. By my golden—what's the
richest thing about me?   125

DILDO.

Your teeth.

BALURDO.

By my golden teeth, hold up, that I may put in; hold up,
I say, that I may see to put on my gloves.

DILDO.

O delicious sweet-cheek'd master, if you discharge but one
glance from the level of that set face, O, you will strike a   130
wench; you'll make any wench love you.

BALURDO.

By Jesu, I think I am as elegant a courtier as—How lik'st
thou my suit?

DILDO.

All, beyond all, no peregal; you are wonder'd at [*aside*] for
an ass.   135

117. More fools] *This edn.;* more   134. S.P. DILDO.] *This edn.; Catz. Q.*
foole *Q.*

---

116. *potato pie*] believed to be an aphrodisiac.
119. *plot*] the playhouse synopsis of the action.
121. *loofe*] perhaps the dialect word for "hand."
122. *God's neaks*] meaningless oath.
123. *Curson*] dialect word for "Christian."   124. *girn*] grimace.
130. *level*] the position of taking aim.   134. *peregal*] equal.

BALURDO.

Well, Dildo; no Christian creature shall know hereafter
what I will do for thee heretofore.

ROSSALINE.

Here wants a little white, Flavia.

DILDO.

Ay, but master, you have one little fault: you sleep open-
mouth'd.   140

BALURDO.

Pew, thou jest'st. In good sadness, I'll have a looking glass
nail'd to the testern of the bed, that I may see when I sleep
whether 'tis so or not; take heed you lie not; go to, take heed
you lie not.

FLAVIA.

By my troth you look as like the Princess now—   145

ROSSALINE.

Ay, but her lip is—lip is a little—redder, a very little redder.
But by the help of Art or Nature, ere I change my periwig
mine shall be as red.

FLAVIA.

O, ay, that face, that eye, that smile, that writhing of your
body, that wanton dandling of your fan, becomes prethily, 150
so sweethly; [Rossaline *gives her money*] 'tis even the goodest
lady that breathes, the most amiable—faith, the fringe of
your satin petticoat is ripp'd. Good faith, madam, they say
you are the most bounteous lady to your women that ever—
[*Gives more money.*] O most delicious beauty! Good madam, 155
let me kith it.

Enter Piero.

FELICHE.

Rare sport, rare sport! A female fool and a female flatterer.

ROSSALINE.

Body o' me, the Duke! away the glass!

PIERO.

Take up your paper, Rossaline.

142. the testern] *Halliwell;* the the   146. S.P. ROSSALINE.] *This edn.;*
testern *Q*.   *speech continued to Flavia in Q.*

142. *testern*] canopy.
150–156. *prethily . . . sweethly . . . kith*] Flavia has aquired a lisp.

ROSSALINE.

Not mine, my lord.   160

PIERO.

Not yours, my lady? I'll see what 'tis.

BALURDO.

And how does my sweet mistress? O lady dear, even as 'tis
an old say: 'tis an old horse can neither wehee nor wag his
tail; even so do I hold my set face still; even so 'tis a bad
courtier that can neither discourse nor blow his nose.   165

PIERO [reads].

"*Meet me at Abraham's, the Jew's, where I bought my Amazon's
disguise. A ship lies in the port, ready bound for England. Make
haste; come private.* Antonio."

Forobosco, Alberto, Feliche, Castilio, Balurdo!

Enter Castilio, Forobosco, [Alberto].

Run, keep the palace, post to the ports, go to my daughter's 170
chamber. Whither now? scud to the Jew's; stay, run to the
gates; stop the gondolets; let none pass the marsh; do all at
once. Antonio his head, his head! Keep you the court; the
rest stand still, or run, or go, or shout, or search, or scud, or
call, or hang, or do–do–do, so–so–so–something. I know not 175
who–who–who–what I do–do–do–nor who–who–who–where
I am.   [*Exeunt all save* Piero, Feliche.]

O trista traditrice, rea, ribalda fortuna,

Negandomi vendetta mi causa fera morte.   [*Exit.*]

FELICHE.

Ha, ha, ha. I could break my spleen at his impatience.   180

[*Enter* Antonio *below and* Mellida *above.*]

ANTONIO.

Alma e graziosa fortuna siate favorevole,

168. Antonio.] *Halliwell; printed at*   169.1.] *Printed after* private, *l. 168 Q.*
beginning of l. 169 in Q.

---

163. *say*] saw, saying.   163. *wehee*] whinny (cf. Tilley, 671).
172. *gondolets*] gondolas.
178–179. *O trista . . . morte*] "O ruffian Fortune, condemned and wretched
traitress, by denying my revenge you cause me beastly death."
181–182. *Alma e . . . Mellida.*] "Kind and gracious Fortune, be favorable
to me; and may the vows of my dear Mellida be fortunate."

E fortunati siano i vuoti della mia dolce Mellida, Mellida.

MELLIDA.

Alas, Antonio, I have lost thy note.

A number mount my stairs; I'll straight return.   [*Exit.*]

[Antonio *falls to the ground.*]

FELICHE.

Antonio,   185
Be not affright, sweet prince; appease thy fear;
Buckle thy spirits up; put all thy wits
In wimble action, or thou art surpris'd.

ANTONIO.

I care not.

FELICHE.

Art mad or desperate, or—   190

ANTONIO.

Both, both, all, all. I pray thee let me lie;
Spite of you all, I can and I will die.

FELICHE.

You are distraught; O, this is madness' breath.

ANTONIO.

Each man takes hence life, but no man death;
He's a good fellow and keeps open house;   195
A thousand thousand ways lead to his gate,
To his wide-mouth'd porch; when niggard life
Hath but one little, little wicket through.
We wring ourselves into this wretched world
To pule and weep, exclaim, to curse and rail,   200
To fret and ban the fates, to strike the earth
As I do now. Antonio, curse thy birth,
And die.

FELICHE.

Nay, heaven's my comfort, now you are perverse;

---

182. *i vuoti della mia dolce Mellida,*   *Mellida, Mellida Q.*
Mellida] *This edn.; vuoti del mia dulce*   194. takes] *Bullen; take Q.*

183. *note*] as above, ll.166–168.
184. *A number . . . stairs*] She hears people climbing the stairs to her
chamber (i.e., to the upper stage).
188. *wimble*] nimble.
194.] from Seneca *Phoenissae* 152.

You know I always lov'd you; pray thee live;   205
Wilt thou strike dead thy friends, draw mourning tears?

ANTONIO.

Alas, Feliche, I ha' ne'er a friend,
No country, father, brother, kinsman left
To weep my fate or sigh my funeral;
I roll but up and down, and fill a seat   210
In the dark cave of dusky misery.

FELICHE.

'Fore heaven, the Duke comes! Hold you; take my key;
Slink to my chamber; look you, that is it.
There shall you find a suit I wore at sea;
Take it and slip away. Nay, precious!   215
If you'll be peevish, by this light I'll swear
Thou rail'dst upon thy love before thou diedst
And call'd her strumpet.

ANTONIO.   She'll not credit thee.

FELICHE.

Tut, that's all one. I'll defame thy love,
And make thy dead trunk held in vile regard.   220

ANTONIO.

Wilt needs have it so? Why then, Antonio:
Vive speranza in despetto dell fato.   [*Exit.*]

Enter Piero, Galeatzo, Matzagente, Forobosco, Balurdo, *and* Castilio,
with weapons.

PIERO.

O my sweet princes, was't not bravely found?
Even there I found the note; even there it lay.
I kiss the place for joy that there it lay.   225
This way he went; here let us make a stand;
I'll keep this gate myself. O gallant youth!
I'll drink carouse unto your country's health,
Even in Antonio's skull.

BALURDO.

Lord bless us! His breath is more fearful than a sergeant's   230
voice, when he cries, "I arrest."

---

222. *Vive ... fato*] "Hope lives in spite of Fate."
230. *sergeant*] the officer who arrested offenders.

Enter Antonio [*disguised as a sailor*].

ANTONIO.

Stop Antonio; keep, keep Antonio!

PIERO.

Where, where, man, where?

ANTONIO.

Here, here; let me—me pursue him down the marsh.

PIERO.

Hold; there's my signet; take a gondolet.   235
Bring me his head, his head, and by mine honor,
I'll make thee the wealthiest mariner that breathes.

ANTONIO.

I'll sweat my blood out till I have him safe.   [*Exit.*]

PIERO.

Spoke heartily i' faith, good mariner.
O, we will mount in triumph; soon, at night,   240
I'll set his head up. Let's think where.

BALURDO.

Upon his shoulders; that's the fittest place for it. If it be not
as fit as if it were made for them, say, "Balurdo, thou art a
sot, an ass."

Enter Mellida *in page's attire, dancing.*

PIERO.

Sprightly, i' faith. In truth, he's somewhat like   245
My daughter Mellida; but alas, poor soul,
Her honor heels, God knows, are half so light.

MELLIDA.

Escap'd I am, spite of my father's spite.   [*Exit.*]

PIERO.

Ho, this will warm my bosom ere I sleep.

Enter Flavia, *running.*

FLAVIA.

O my lord, your daughter!   250

PIERO.

Ay, ay, my daughter's safe enough, I warrant thee.
This vengeance on the boy will lengthen out

231.1. *Enter* Antonio] *Bullen; after*   239. Spoke] *Bullen;* speake *Q.*
l. 228 in Q.

–49–

My days unmeasuredly.
It shall be chronicled, time to come:
Piero Sforza slew Andrugio's son.   255
FLAVIA.
   Ay but my lord, your daughter—
PIERO.
   Ay, ay, my good wench, she is safe enough.
FLAVIA.
   O then, my lord, you know she's run away.
PIERO.
   Run away, away; how run away?
FLAVIA.
   She's vanish'd in an instant, none knows whither.   260
PIERO.
   Pursue, pursue, fly, run post, scud away!

     Feliche *sings*, "And was not good King Solomon."

   Fly, call, run, row, ride, cry, shout, hurry, haste;
   Haste, hurry, shout, cry, ride, row, run, call, fly;
   Backward and forward, every way about.
   Maledetta fortuna che con dura sorta . . .   265
   Che farò, che dirò, per fugir tanto mal?
         [*Exeunt all save* Castilio, Feliche.]
CASTILIO.
   'Twas you that struck me even now, was it not?
FELICHE.
   It was I that struck you even now.
CASTILIO.
   You bastinadoed me, I take it.
FELICHE.
   I bastinadoed you, and you took it.   270
CASTILIO.
   Faith sir, I have the richest tobacco in the court for you; I
   would be glad to make you satisfaction if I have wronged

266. *per*] *This edn.; pur Q.*

---

261. *run post*] run express.
265–266. *Maledetta . . . tanto mal*] "Malicious fortune, which with harsh
lottery . . . What shall I do, what shall I say, to escape so great an evil?"
269. *bastinadoed*] beat.

you. I would not the sun should set upon your anger; give
me your hand.

FELICHE.

    Content, faith, so thou'lt breed no more such lies.   275
    I hate not man, but man's lewd qualities.   [*Exeunt.*]

[IV.i]   *Enter* Antonio *in his sea-gown, running.*

ANTONIO [*calling aloud*].

    Stop; stop Antonio; stay Antonio.
    [*To himself.*] Vain breath, vain breath; Antonio's lost;
    He cannot find himself, not seize himself.
    Alas, this that you see is not Antonio;
    His spirit hovers in Piero's court,   5
    Hurling about his agile faculties
    To apprehend the sight of Mellida.
    But poor, poor soul, wanting apt instruments
    To speak or see, stands dumb and blind, sad spirit,
    Roll'd up in gloomy clouds as black as air   10
    Through which the rusty coach of night is drawn.
    'Tis so; I'll give you instance that 'tis so;
    Conceit you me: as, having clasp'd a rose
    Within my palm, the rose being ta'en away,
    My hand retains a little breath of sweet;   15
    So may man's trunk; his spirit slipp'd away,
    Holds still a faint perfume of his sweet guest.
    'Tis so; for when discursive powers fly out
    And roam in progress through the bounds of heaven,
    The soul itself gallops along with them   20
    As chieftain of this winged troop of thought;
    Whilst the dull lodge of spirit standeth waste
    Until the soul return from—What was't I said?
    O, this is naught but speckling melancholy.
    I have been—   25

---

273. *I . . . anger*] from Ephesians 4:26.
[IV.i]
    0.1. *sea-gown*] i.e., the suit which Feliche offered him at III.ii.214.
    11. *rusty coach of night*] cf. Marlowe, *I Tamburlaine*, 2075 and *Edward II*,
1739.
    13. *Conceit*] understand.   24. *speckling*] darkening.

That Morpheus tender skinp—Cousin german—
Bear with me good—
Mellida—Clod upon clod thus fall.   [*Falls to the ground.*]
Hell is beneath; yet Heaven is over all.

Enter Andrugio, Lucio [*and* page].

ANDRUGIO.

Come Lucio; let's go eat; what hast thou got?   30
Roots? Roots? Alas, they are seeded, new cut up.
O, thou hast wronged nature, Lucio;
But boots not much; thou but pursu'st the world,
That cuts off virtue 'fore it comes to growth
Lest it should seed and so o'errun her son,   35
Dull purblind Error. Give me water, boy;
There is no poison in't I hope; they say
That lurks in massy plate; and yet the earth
Is so infected with a general plague
That he's most wise that thinks there's no man fool,   40
Right prudent that esteems no creature just;
Great policy the least things to mistrust.
Give me assay. [*They eat.*] How we mock greatness now!

LUCIO.

A strong conceit is rich, so most men deem;
If not to be, 'tis comfort yet to seem.   45

ANDRUGIO.

Why man, I never was a prince till now.
'Tis not the bared pate, the bended knees,
Gilt tipstaves, Tyrian purple, chairs of state,
Troops of pied butterflies that flutter still
In greatness' summer, that confirm a prince;   50

29.1.] *Bullen; Enter Andrugio, Lucio,*
Cole, and Norwod. Q.

---

28. *Clod . . . fall*] Let one clod (Antonio) fall down on another (the earth).
29.1. *Enter . . . Lucio*] The additional names in Q (see textual note) may be those of actors.
31. *they . . . up*] those that you have newly cut up had begun to germinate.
33. *pursu'st the world*] do the same as everyone else.
37. *they say*] i.e., Seneca (in *Thyestes* 453).
43. *assay*] tasting the food before a nobleman eats.
46–66.] Imitated from Seneca *Thyestes* 342 ff.
48. *tipstaves*] ceremonial sticks carried by officials.

'Tis not the unsavory breath of multitudes
Shouting and clapping with confused din
That makes a prince. No, Lucio, he's a king,
A true right king, that dares do aught save wrong,
Fears nothing mortal but to be unjust;   55
Who is not blown up with the flattering puffs
Of spongy sycophants, who stands unmov'd
Despite the justling of opinion,
Who can enjoy himself maugre the throng
That strive to press his quiet out of him,   60
Who sits upon Jove's footstool, as I do,
Adoring, not affecting, majesty,
Whose brow is wreathed with the silver crown
Of clear content. This, Lucio, is a king,
And of this empire every man's possess'd   65
That's worth his soul.

LUCIO.
My lord, the Genoese had wont to say—

ANDRUGIO.
Name not the Genoese; that very word
Unkings me quite, makes me vile passion's slave.
O you that made open the glibbery ice   70
Of vulgar favor, view Andrugio:
Was never prince with more applause confirm'd,
With louder shouts of triumph launched out
Into the surgy main of government;
Was never prince with more despite cast out,   75
Left shipwreck'd, banish'd, on more guiltless ground.
O rotten props of the craz'd multitude, how you
Still double, falter under the lightest chance
That strains your veins. Alas, one battle lost,
Your whorish love, your drunken healths, your hoots and

---

57. *spongy*] deficient in solidity.
58. *opinion*] Stoic technical term for irrational sense-impression.
59. *maugre*] in spite of.   65.] From *Thyestes* 390.
70. *made open*] broke the ice, for others to follow.
70. *glibbery*] slippery.
76. *on more guiltless ground*] with less just cause (with pun on *ground* = shore).
78. *double*] bend over.

shouts,   80
Your smooth "God save's," and all your devils, last,
That tempts our quiet to your hell of throngs—
Spit on me, Lucio, for I am turn'd slave;
Observe how passion domineers o'er me.

LUCIO.
No wonder, noble lord, having lost a son,   85
A country, crown, and—

ANDRUGIO.
Ay, Lucio, having lost a son, a son,
A country, house, crown, son. *O lares, miseri lares!*
Which shall I first deplore? My son, my son,
My dear sweet boy, my dear Antonio.   90

ANTONIO.
Antonio?

ANDRUGIO.
Ay, echo, ay; I mean Antonio.

ANTONIO.
Antonio? Who means Antonio?

ANDRUGIO.
Where art? What art? Know'st thou Antonio?

ANTONIO.
Yes.   95

ANDRUGIO.
Lives he?

ANTONIO.
No.

ANDRUGIO.
Where lies he dead?

ANTONIO.
Here.

ANDRUGIO.
Where?   100

ANTONIO.
Here.   [*Raising himself.*]

88. *miseri*] Bullen; *misereri* Q.

---

88. *house*] dynasty.
88. *O lares, miseri lares*] "O household gods, ye wretched household
gods!"

ANDRUGIO.
Art thou Antonio?

ANTONIO.
I think I am.

ANDRUGIO.
Dost thou but think? What, dost not know thyself?

ANTONIO.
He is a fool that thinks he knows himself. 105

ANDRUGIO.
Upon thy faith to heaven, give thy name.

ANTONIO.
I were not worthy of Andrugio's blood
If I denied my name's Antonio.

ANDRUGIO.
I were not worthy to be call'd thy father
If I denied my name Andrugio. 110
And dost thou live? O, let me kiss thy cheek
And dew thy brow with trickling drops of joy.
Now Heaven's will be done, for I have liv'd
To see my joy, my son Antonio.
Give me thy hand; now, Fortune, do thy worst; 115
His blood, that lapp'd thy spirit in the womb,
Thus, in his love, will make his arms thy tomb. [*They embrace.*]

ANTONIO.
Bless not the body with your twining arms
Which is accurst of heaven. O, what black sin
Hath been committed by our ancient house, 120
Whose scalding vengeance lights upon our heads,
That thus the world and fortune casts us out
As loathed objects, Ruin's branded slaves.

ANDRUGIO.
Do not expostulate the heavens' will.
But, O, remember to forget thyself; 125
Forget remembrance what thou once hast been.
Come, creep with me from out this open air;
Even trees have tongues and will betray our life.

124. *expostulate*] complain about.

−55−

I am a-raising of our house, my boy,
Which Fortune will not envy, 'tis so mean   130
And like the world, all dirt; there shalt thou rip
The inwards of thy fortunes in mine ears
Whilst I sit weeping, blind with passion's tears;
Then I'll begin, and we'll such order keep,
That one shall still tell griefs, the other weep.   135

       Exit Andrugio [*and* Lucio], *leaving* Antonio *and his* page.

ANTONIO.

I'll follow you. Boy, pray thee stay a little.
Thou hast had a good voice, if this cold marsh,
Wherein we lurk, have not corrupted it.

Enter Mellida, *standing out of sight, in her page's suit.*

I pray thee sing, but sirrah, mark you me,
Let each note breathe the heart of passion,   140
The sad extracture of extremest grief.
Make me a strain; speak groaning like a bell
That tolls departing souls.
Breathe me a point that may enforce me weep,
To wring my hands, to break my cursed breast,   145
Rave and exclaim, lie groveling on the earth,
Straight start up frantic, crying, "Mellida."
Sing but, "Antonio hath lost Mellida,"
And thou shalt see me, like a man possess'd,
Howl out such passion that even this brinish marsh   150
Will squeeze out tears from out his spongy cheeks,
The rocks even groan, and—
Pray thee, pray thee sing,
Or I shall ne'er ha' done; when I am in,
'Tis harder for me end than to begin.   155

The boy *runs a note;* Antonio *breaks it.*

---

129. *our house*] a mud hovel on the stage (with secondary reference to
house=dynasty).
135.1. *his*] i.e., Andrugio's.
141. *extracture*] essence.   142. *a strain*] a song.
144. *point*] note.   154. *in*] in the vein.
155.1. *runs a note*] prolongs one syllable in singing.

For look thee boy, my grief that hath no end
I may begin to plain, but—Pray thee sing.

Cantant.

MELLIDA.

Heaven keep you, sir.

ANTONIO.

Heaven keep you from me, sir.

MELLIDA.

I must be acquainted with you, sir.   160

ANTONIO.

Wherefore? Art thou infected with misery,
Sear'd with the anguish of calamity?
Art thou true sorrow, hearty grief; canst weep?
I am not for thee if thou canst not rave,

Antonio *falls on the ground.*

Fall flat on the ground, and thus exclaim on heaven: 165
"O trifling Nature, why inspiredst thou breath?"

MELLIDA.

Stay sir, I think you named Mellida.

ANTONIO.

Know'st thou Mellida?

MELLIDA.
Yes.

ANTONIO.

Hast thou seen Mellida?   170

MELLIDA.
Yes.

ANTONIO.

Then hast thou seen the glory of her sex,
The music of nature, the unequal'd luster
Of unmatched excellence, the united sweet
Of heaven's graces, the most adored beauty   175
That ever struck amazement in the world.

MELLIDA.

You seem to love her.

ANTONIO.

With my very soul.

157.1. *Cantant*] "They sing."

MELLIDA.

  She'll not requite it; all her love is fix'd
  Upon a gallant, one Antonio,   180
  The Duke of Genoa's son. I was her page;
  And often as I waited, she would sigh,
  "O dear Antonio," and to strengthen thought
  Would clip my neck and kiss, and kiss me thus. [*Kisses him.*]
  Therefore leave loving her; fa, faith, methinks   185
  Her beauty is not half so ravishing
  As you discourse of; she hath a freckled face,
  A low forehead and a lumpish eye.

ANTONIO.

  O Heaven, that I should hear such blasphemy!
  Boy, rogue, thou liest, and—   [*Recognizes* Mellida.] 190
  Spavento del mio core, dolce Mellida,
  Di grave morte ristoro vero, dolce Mellida,
  Celeste salvatrice, sovrana Mellida
  Del mio sperar; trofeo vero Mellida.

MELLIDA.

  Diletta e soave anima mia Antonio,   195
  Godevole bellezza, cortese Antonio.
  Signior mio e virginal amore bell' Antonio,
  Gusto dei miei sensi, car' Antonio.

180. one] *1633;* on *Q.*

---

188. *lumpish*] dull and heavy.

191–208. *Spavento . . . morir*] Terror of my heart, sweet Mellida, true medicine against sad death, sweet Mellida, heavenly savior, Mellida, sovereign of my hope, true trophy, Mellida.

Mellida. Antonio, my chosen and delightful soul,
Courteous Antonio, delightful in beauty,
Fair Antonio, my lord and love of my virginity,
Dear Antonio, food for my affections.
 Antonio. O dissolve my heart in a sweet kiss.
 Mellida. Let the senses die in fulfilled desire.
 Antonio. Can there be a purer good in heaven?
 Mellida. Can there be a purer good on earth?
 Antonio. Give me a kiss from your blessed mouth.
Let me gather up the perfumed air which nests up there in these sweet lips.
 Mellida. Give me the empire of thy consenting love
Which blesses me, with an eternal honor,
For true, thus it is fit that I should die.

ANTONIO.

O svanisce il cor in un soave bacio.

MELLIDA.

Muoiono i sensi nel desiato desio. 200

ANTONIO.

Nel Cielo può esser beltà più chiara?

MELLIDA.

Nel mondo può esser beltà più chiara?

ANTONIO.

Dammi un bacio da quella bocca beata.
Lasciami coglier l'aura odorata
Che in sù anneggia, in quelle dolci labbra. 205

MELLIDA.

Dammi l'impero del tuo gradit' amore,
Che bea me, con sempiterno onore,
Così così, mi converrà morir.
Good sweet, scout o'er the marsh, for my heart trembles
At every little breath that strikes my ear 210
[. . . . .]
When thou returnest; and I'll discourse
How I deceiv'd the court; then thou shall tell
How thou escap'dst the watch; we'll point our speech
With amorous kissing, kissing commas, and even suck
The liquid breath from out each other's lips. 215

ANTONIO [*to himself, going*].

Dull clod, no man but such sweet favor clips.
I go, and yet my panting blood persuades me stay.
Turn coward in her sight? Away, away. [*Exit.*]

199. *svanisce*] *Bullen; suamisce Q.*
200. *Muoiono*] *Bullen; Murono Q.*
201,202. *più*] *Bullen; pia Q.*
201. *può esser*] *Bullen; puo lesser Q.*
202. *può esser*] *Bullen; pol esser Q.*
204. *Lasciami*] *Bullen; Bassiami Q.*
205. *in sù anneggia*] *This edn.; in sua neggia Q.*

206. *l'impero*] *This edn.; pimpero Q.*
207. *con sempiterno*] *Bullen; cosempiterno Q.*
following line 210] *some words are apparently missing from the text of Q at this point.*

213. *point*] punctuate.
214. *kissing commas*] they will kiss at every comma.
216. *Dull . . . clips*] Poor-spirited creature (reluctant to leave), don't you know that the delights of love are common to all men.

PAGE.

I think confusion of Babel is fall'n upon these lovers, that
they change their language; but I fear me my master, 220
having but feigned the person of a woman, hath got their
unfeigned imperfection and is grown double tongu'd. As
for Mellida, she were no woman if she could not yield strange
language. But howsoever, if I should sit in judgment, 'tis an
error easier to be pardoned by the auditors' than excused 225
by the author's; and yet some private respect may rebate
the edge of the keener censure.   [*Exit.*]

Enter Piero, Castilio, Matzagente, Forobosco, Feliche, Galeatzo,
[*at one door*]; Balurdo *and his page* [Dildo], *at another door.*

PIERO.

This way she took; search, my sweet gentlemen.
How now, Balurdo, canst thou meet with anybody?

BALURDO.

As I am true gentleman I made my horse sweat that he hath 230
ne'er a dry thread on him; and I can meet with no living
creature but men and beasts. In good sadness I would have
sworn I had seen Mellida even now; for I saw a thing stir
under a hedge and I peep'd and I spied a thing; and I
peer'd and I tweer'd underneath, and truly a right wise man 235
might have been deceived, for it was—

PIERO.

What, in the name of heaven?

BALURDO.

A dun cow.

FELICHE.

Sh'ad ne'er a kettle on her head?

PIERO [*to* Mellida].

Boy, didst thou see a young lady pass this way?   240

219. S.P. PAGE.] *Bullen; speech con-
tinues to Antonio Q.*

224–227. '*tis . . . censure*] This fault (of writing in Italian) is easier for the
audience to forgive than the author to justify; yet strong objection may be
tempered for some personal reasons.
235. *tweer'd*] peeped (OED *twire*).
239. *a kettle*] Guy of Warwick had a dun cow and a kettle; Marston is
probably remembering an inn sign.

GALEATZO.

Why speak you not?

BALURDO.

God's neaks, proud elf, give the Duke reverence; stand bare,
with a—[*Knocks her cap off.*] Whogh! Heavens bless me—
Mellida, Mellida!

PIERO.

Where man, where?   245

BALURDO.

Turn'd man, turn'd man; women wear the breeches; lo
here!

PIERO.

Light and unduteous! Kneel not, peevish elf;
Speak not, entreat not, shame unto my house,
Curse to my honor. Where's Antonio,   250
Thou traitress to my hate? What, is he shipp'd
For England now? Well, whimpering harlot, hence!

MELLIDA.

Good father—

PIERO.

Good me no goods. Seest thou that sprightly youth?
Ere thou canst term tomorrow morning old   255
Thou shalt call him thy husband, lord and love.

MELLIDA.

Ay me!

PIERO.

Blirt on your ay me's! Guard her safely hence.
Drag her away. I'll be your guard tonight.
Young prince, mount up your spirits and prepare   260
To solemnize your nuptial's eve with pomp.

GALEATZO.

The time is scant; now nimble wits appear;
Phoebus begins to gleam, the welkin's clear.

                Exeunt all but Balurdo *and his page* [Dîldo].

263. to] *1633; not in* Q.

242. *give . . . reverence*] Commoners stood bareheaded before nobility.
258. *Blirt*] an expletive = blow, blast.
263. *welkin*] sky.

BALURDO.

"Now nimble wits appear": I'll myself appear;
Balurdo's self, that in quick wit doth surpass, 265
Will show the substance of a complete—

DILDO.

Ass, Ass.

BALURDO.

I'll mount my courser and most gallantly prick—

DILDO.

"Gallantly prick" is too long, and stands hardly in the
verse, sir. 270

BALURDO.

I'll speak pure rhyme and will so bravely prank it
That I'll toss love like a—prank—prank it—a rhyme for
"prank it"?

DILDO.

Blanket.

BALURDO.

That I'll toss love like a dog in a blanket. Ha, ha, indeed, la; 275
I think—ha, ha, I think—ha, ha, I think I shall tickle the
Muses. And I strike it not dead, say, "Balurdo, thou art an
arrant sot."

DILDO.

Balurdo, thou art an arrant sot. [*Exeunt.*]

[IV.ii]

Enter Andrugio *and* Antonio *wreathed together,* Lucio [*and* page].

ANDRUGIO.

Now come, united force of chapfall'n death,
Come, power of fretting anguish, leave distress.
O, thus enfolded, we have breasts of proof
'Gainst all the venom'd stings of misery.

ANTONIO.

Father, now I have an antidote 5

276–277. *tickle the Muses*] arouse the spirit of poetry.
[IV.ii]
1. *chapfall'n*] with the jaw fallen open.
2. *leave distress*] ? abandon (as less worthy objects) those who are
distressed by you.

'Gainst all the poison that the world can breathe;
My Mellida, my Mellida doth bless
This bleak waste with her presence. [*To* page.] How now, boy,
Why dost thou weep? Alas, where's Mellida?

PAGE.

Ay me, my lord.   10

ANTONIO.

A sudden horror doth invade my blood;
My sinews tremble and my panting heart
Scuds round about my bosom to go out,
Dreading the assailant, horrid passion.
O, be no tyrant; kill me with one blow;   15
Speak quickly, briefly, boy.

PAGE.

Her father found and seiz'd her; she is gone.

ANDRUGIO.

Son, heat thy blood; be not froze up with grief.
Courage, sweet boy, sink not beneath the weight
Of crushing mischief. O, where's thy dauntless heart,   20
Thy father's spirit? I renounce thy blood,
If thou forsake thy valor.

LUCIO.

See how his grief speaks in his slow-pac'd steps;
Alas, 'tis more than he can utter; let him go:
Dumb solitary path best suiteth woe.   25

ANDRUGIO.

Give me my arms, my armor, Lucio.

LUCIO.

Dear lord, what means this rage? When lacking use
Scarce saves your life, will you in armor rise?

ANDRUGIO.

Fortune fears valor, presseth ˇcowardice.

LUCIO.

Then valor gets applause when it hath place   30

10. S.P. PAGE.] *Bullen; Ant. Q.*   11. S.P. ANTONIO.] *Bullen; And. Q.*

27. *lacking use*] not wearing the armor that identifies one.
29. *presseth*] oppresseth (line from Seneca *Medea* 159).
30–31. *Then . . . blaze it*] i.e., valor is praised only in those whose position gives them scope for its display (paraphrase of Seneca *Medea* 160).

And means to blaze it.

ANDRUGIO.

Numquam potest non esse.

LUCIO.

Patience, my lord, may bring your ills some end.

ANDRUGIO.

What patience, friend, can ruin'd hopes attend?
Come, let me die like old Andrugio,   35
Worthy my birth. O, blood-true-honor'd graves
Are far more blessed than base life of slaves.   *Exeunt.*

[V.i]   *Enter* Balurdo, *a painter with two pictures, and* Dildo.

BALURDO.

And are you a painter, sir? Can you draw, can you draw?

PAINTER.

Yes sir.

BALURDO.

Indeed la! Now so can my father's fore-horse. And are these
the workmanship of your hands?

PAINTER.

I did limn them.   5

BALURDO.

"Limn them"? a good word, "limn them." Whose picture
is this? [*Reads.*] "*Anno Domini* 1599." Believe me, master
Anno Domini was of a good settled age when you limn'd
him; 1599 years old! Let's see the other. [*Reads.*] "*Aetatis suae*
24." By'r Lady, he is somewhat younger. Belike master   10
Aetatis suae was *Anno Domini's* son.

PAINTER.

Is not your master a—

DILDO.

He hath a little proclivity to him.

---

32. *Numquam . . . esse*] the first half of a tag from Seneca *Medea* 161: "a
place for valor can never be lacking."
36. *blood-true-honor'd*] truly honored by the noble shedding of blood.
[V.i]
3. *fore-horse*] the first horse in a team (which "draws" a cart).
9–10. *Aetatis suae 24*] in the twenty-fourth year of his age.
13. *proclivity*] tendency.

PAINTER.

"Proclivity," good youth? I thank you for your courtly
"proclivity."   15

BALURDO.

Approach, good sir. I did send for you to draw me a device,
an *impresa*, by synecdoche, a mott. By Phoebus' crimson
taffeta mantle, I think I speak as melodiously—look you sir,
how think you on't? I would have you paint me for my
device a good fat leg of ewe mutton swimming in stew'd   20
broth of plums—boy, keel your mouth; it runs over—and
the word shall be: "Hold my dish whilst I spill my pottage."
Sure, in my conscience, 'twould be the most sweet device
now.

PAINTER.

'Twould scent of kitchen-stuff too much.   25

BALURDO.

God's neaks, now I remember me, I ha' the rarest device in
my head that ever breathed. Can you paint me a driveling,
reeling song, and let the word be, "Uh."

PAINTER.

A belch?

BALURDO.

O, no, no; "uh"; paint me "uh" or nothing.   30

PAINTER.

It cannot be done, sir, but by a seeming kind of drunkenness.

BALURDO.

No? Well, let me have a good massy ring with your own
posy graven in it, that must sing a small treble, word for
word, thus:

> *And if you will my true lover be*   35
> *Come follow me to the greenwood.*

16–17. *a device, an impresa*] an emblematic picture, often with a motto.
17. *by synecdoche*] making a part stand for the whole.
17. *mott*] a motto.
18. *mantle*] the sun's flames.
21. *keel*] wipe.   22. *word*] motto.
31. *seeming*] visually expressive.
33. *posy*] the motto graven inside a ring.
35–36. *And . . . greenwood*] lines from two popular songs: (1) "How should
I your true love know"; (2) "Hey jolly Robin" (F. W. Sternfeld).

PAINTER.

O Lord, sir, I cannot make a picture sing.

BALURDO.

Why? 'Slid, I have seen painted things sing as sweet But
I have't will tickle it for a conceit, i' faith.

Enter Feliche *and* Alberto.

ALBERTO.

O dear Feliche, give me thy device;   40
How shall I purchase love of Rossaline?

FELICHE.

'Swill, flatter her soundly.

ALBERTO.

Her love is such I cannot flatter her;
But with my utmost vehemence of speech
I have ador'd her beauties.   45

FELICHE.

Hast writ good moving unaffected rhymes to her?

ALBERTO.

O yes, Feliche, but she scorns my writ.

FELICHE.

Hast thou presented her with sumptuous gifts?

ALBERTO.

Alas, my fortunes are too weak to offer them.

FELICHE.

O, then I have it; I'll tell thee what to do.   50

ALBERTO.

What, good Feliche?

FELICHE.

Go and hang thyself; I say, go hang thyself,
If that thou canst not give, go hang thyself.
I'll rhyme thee dead, or verse thee to the rope;
How thinkst thou of a poet that sung thus: 55

---

38. *painted things*] court ladies.

40. *device*] advice.

42. *'Swill*] i.e., God's will.

54. *verse . . . rope*] reference to the "neck-verse" of those pleading Benefit
of Clergy.

Munera sola pacant, sola addunt munera formam;
Munere solicites Pallada, Cypris erit.
Munera, munera?

ALBERTO.

I'll go and breathe my woes unto the rocks,
And spend my grief upon the deafest seas.   60
I'll weep my passion to the senseless trees
And load most solitary air with plaints.
For woods, trees, sea or rocky Appenine
Is not so ruthless as my Rossaline.
Farewell, dear friend, expect no more of me;   65
Here ends my part in this love's comedy.

Exit Alberto *and* Painter.

FELICHE.

Now, Master Balurdo, whither are you going, ha?

BALURDO.

Signior Feliche, how do you, faith, and by my troth, how do
you?

FELICHE.

Whither art thou going, bully?   70

BALURDO.

And as heaven help me, how do you? How do you i' faith,
hee?

FELICHE.

Whither art going, man?

BALURDO.

O God, to the court; I'll be willing to give you grace and
good count'nance, if I may but see you in the presence.   75

FELICHE.

O, to court? Farewell.

BALURDO.

If you see one in a yellow taffeta doublet cut upon carnation
velour, a green hat, a blue pair of velvet hose, a gilt rapier
and an orange-tawny pair of worsted silk stockings, that's I,

---

56–58. *Munera . . . Munera, munera*] "Tis gifts alone subdue, gifts alone
add beauty; if you solicit the goddess of wisdom with a gift, she will become
a Venus. Gifts, gifts" (not traced; not classical).
63–64. *For . . . Rossaline*] reminiscence of *As You Like It*, III.ii. 78 ff.
74–75. *grace and good count'nance*] favor and assistance.

that's I. 80

FELICHE.

Very good; farewell.

BALURDO.

Ho, you shall know me as easily; I ha' bought me a new
green feather with a red sprig; you shall see my wrought
shirt hang out at my breeches; you shall know me.

FELICHE.

Very good, very good; farewell. 85

BALURDO.

Marry, in the masque 'twill be somewhat hard. But if you
hear anybody speak so wittily that he makes all the room
laugh, that's I, that's I. Farewell, good signior. [*Exeunt.*]

[V.ii]

Enter Forobosco, Castilio, *a* boy *carrying a gilt harp,* Piero, Mellida
in night apparel, Rossaline, Flavia, two pages.

PIERO.

Advance the music's prize; now cap'ring wits
Rise to your highest mount; let choice delight
Garland the brow of this triumphant night.

FOROBOSCO.

'Sfoot, 'a sits like Lucifer himself.

ROSSALINE.

Good sweet Duke, first let their voices strain for music's 5
prize; give me the golden harp; faith, with your favor, I'll
be umpiress.

PIERO.

Sweet niece, content; boys, clear your voice and sing.

1 *Cantat.*

ROSSALINE.

By this gold, I had rather have a servant with a short nose

4. S.P. FOROBOSCO] *This edn.; speech
continued to Piero Q.*

83. *sprig*] an ornament in the form of a spray.
86. *hard*] i.e., hard to know me.
[V.ii]
8.1; 18.1; 23.1. *1,2,3 Cantat*] first (second, third) boy sings.

and a thin hair than have such a high-stretch'd minikin   10
voice.

PIERO.

Fair niece, your reason?

ROSSALINE.

By the sweets of love, I should fear extremely that he were
an eunuch.

CASTILIO.

Spark spirit, how like you his voice?   15

ROSSALINE.

Spark spirit, how like you his voice? So help me, youth, thy
voice squeaks like a dry cork shoe; come, come; let's hear
the next.

2 *Cantat.*

PIERO.

Trust me, a good strong mean. Well sung, my boy.

Enter Balurdo.

BALURDO.

Hold, hold, hold; are ye blind, could you not see my voice   20
coming for the harp? And I knock not division on the head
take hence the harp, make me a slip and let me go but for
ninepence. Sir Mark, strike up for Master Balurdo.

3 *Cantat.*

Judgment, gentlemen, judgment. Was't not above line?
I appeal to your mouths that heard my song.   25
   Do me right, and dub me knight,
   Balurdo.

ROSSALINE.

Kneel down and I'll dub thee knight of the golden harp.

13. sweets] *This edn.;* sweete *Q.*

---

10. *minikin*] shrill. 15. *Spark spirit*] glittering wit.
19. *mean*] counter-tenor.
21. *knock . . . head*] triumph completely in singing descant.
22. *slip*] a counterfeit coin.
24. *above line*] passing the test (? = "over the net" in tennis).
26–27. *Do . . . Balurdo*] a parody of the song "Monsieur Mingo."

BALURDO.

Indeed, la, do; and I'll make you lady of the silver fiddlestick.

ROSSALINE.

Come, kneel, kneel.   30

Enter a page to Balurdo [*to receive the golden harp*].

BALURDO.

My troth, I thank you; it hath never a whistle in't.

ROSSALINE [*to* Mellida].

Nay, good sweet coz, raise up your drooping eyes; and I
were at the point of "To have and to hold, from this day
forward" I would be asham'd to look thus lumpish. What,
my pretty coz, 'tis but the loss of an odd maidenhead. Shall's 35
dance? Thou art so sad, hark in thine ear—I was about to
say—but I'll forbear.

BALURDO [*answering to calls offstage*].

I come, I come. More than most honeysuckle-sweet ladies,
pine not for my presence; I'll return in pomp. Well spoke,
Sir Jeffrey Balurdo. As I am a true knight, I feel honorable 40
eloquence begin to grope me already.   *Exit.*

PIERO.

Faith, mad niece, I wonder when thou wilt marry.

ROSSALINE.

Faith, kind uncle, when men abandon jealousy, forsake
taking of tobacco and cease to wear their beards so rudely
long. O, to have a husband with a mouth continually 45
smoking, with a bush of furze on the ridge of his chin, ready
still to slop into his foaming chaps; ah, 'tis more than most
intolerable.

PIERO.

Nay, faith, sweet niece, I was mighty strong in thought we
should have shut up night with an old comedy: the Prince 50
of Milan shall have Mellida, and thou shouldst have—

ROSSALINE.

Nobody, good sweet uncle. I tell you, sir, I have thirty-nine

36. thine] *Bullen;* mine *Q.*

---

29. *fiddlestick*] *double-entendre.*   31. *it*] the golden harp.
34. *lumpish*] heavy.   42–48. *Faith . . . intolerable.*] Cf. *Much Ado*, II. i. 24 ff.
51. *Milan*] Marston's error for "Florence."

servants and my monkey—that makes the fortieth. Now I
love all of them lightly for something, but affect none of
them seriously for anything. One's a passionate fool and he   55
flatters me above belief; the second's a testy ape and he rails
at me beyond reason; the third's as grave as some censor and
he strokes up his mustachios three times and makes six
plots of set faces before he speaks one wise word; the fourth's
as dry as the bur of an artichoke; the fifth paints and hath   60
always a good color for what he speaks; the sixth—

PIERO.

Stay, stay, sweet niece; what makes you thus suspect young
gallants' worth?

ROSSALINE.

O when I see one wear a periwig I dread his hair; another
wallow in a great slop, I mistrust the proportion of his thigh;   65
and wears a ruffled boot, I fear the fashion of his leg. Thus
something in each thing, one trick in everything, makes me
mistrust imperfection in all parts; and there's the full point
of my addiction.

The cornets sound a sennet. Enter Galeatzo, Matzagente, *and* Balurdo,
in masquery.

PIERO.

The room's too scant; boys, stand in there close.   70
MELLIDA [*to* Galeatzo].

In faith, fair sir, I am too sad to dance.
PIERO.

How's that, how's that? too sad? By heaven, dance,
And grace him too, or—Go to, I say no more.
MELLIDA [*reading the device*].

A burning glass, the word, *Splendente Phoebo;*
'Tis too curious; I conceit it not.   75

---

60. *bur*] a rough berry.   60. *paints*] uses cosmetics.
61. *color*] (1) painted complexion; (2) argument.
65. *great slop*] baggy breeches.
66. *ruffled boot*] top boot with loose turned-over top.
68. *full point*] close, summary.
70. *scant*] small.   74. *word*] motto.
74. *Splendente Phoebo*] "while the sun shines."
75. *curious*] complex.   75. *conceit*] understand.

GALEATZO.

Faith, I'll tell thee. I'll no longer burn than you'll shine and
smile upon my love. For look ye, fairest, by your pure sweets,
I do not dote upon your excellence,
And, faith, unless you shed your brightest beams
Of sunny favor and acceptive grace   80
Upon my tender love, I do not burn.
Marry, but shine and I'll reflect your beams
With fervent ardor.
Faith, I would be loath to flatter thee, fair soul, because I
love, not dote, court like thy husband, which thy father   85
swears tomorrow morn I must be. This is all, and now from
henceforth, trust me Mellida, I'll not speak one wise word
to thee more.

MELLIDA.

I trust ye.

GALEATZO.

By my troth, I'll speak pure fool to thee now.   90

MELLIDA.

You will speak the liker yourself.

GALEATZO.

Good faith, I'll accept of the coxcomb, so you will not refuse
the bauble.

MELLIDA.

Nay, good sweet, keep them both; I am enamor'd of neither.

GALEATZO.

Go to, I must take you down for this. Lend me your ear.   95
                                           [*They walk aside.*]

ROSSALINE [*reading the device*].

A glowworm, the word, *Splendescit tantum tenebris.*

MATZAGENTE.

O lady, the glowworm figurates my valor which shineth
brightest in most dark, dismal and horrid achievements.

ROSSALINE.

Or rather, your glowworm represents your wit which only

---

93. *bauble*] *double-entendre.*
96. **Splendescit** . . . *tenebris*] "It shines only in the dark."

seems to have fire in it, though indeed 'tis but an *ignis fatuus* 100
and shines only in the dark dead night of fools' admiration.

MATZAGENTE.

Lady, my wit hath spurs if it were dispos'd to ride you.

ROSSALINE.

Faith sir, your wit's spurs have but walking rowels; dull,
blunt, they will not draw blood. The gentlemen ushers may
admit them the presence for any wrong they can do to ladies. 105

[*They walk aside.*]

BALURDO.

Truly, I have strained a note above E la for a device; look
you, 'tis a fair rul'd singing book; the word, *Perfect, if it were
prick'd.*

FLAVIA.

Though you are mask'd I can guess who you are by your
wit. You are not the exquisite Balurdo, the most rarely 110
shap'd Balurdo?

BALURDO.

Who, I? No, I am not Sir Jeffrey Balurdo. I am not as well
known by my wit as an alehouse by a red lattice. I am not
worthy to love and be belov'd of Flavia.

FLAVIA.

I will not scorn to favor such good parts as are applauded in 115
your rarest self.

BALURDO.

Truly, you speak wisely, and like a gentlewoman of fourteen
years of age. You know the stone called *lapis*; the nearer it
comes to the fire the hotter it is: and the bird which the
Geometricians call *avis*; the farther it is from the earth the 120
nearer it is to the heaven: and love, the nigher it is to the
flame the more remote—there's a word, "remote"—the more
remote it is from the frost. Your wit is quick, a little thing
pleaseth a young lady, and a small favor contenteth an old

---

100. *ignis fatuus*] will o' the wisp.
103. *walking rowels*] blunt spurs.
106. *above E la*] beyond the highest note in the musical scale.
108. *prick'd*] (of music) written down—with *double-entendre*.
118–123. *You know . . . frost*] parody of Euphuism.
123. *thing*] with *double-entendre*—cf. Tilley, T 189.

courtier; and so, sweet mistress, I truss my codpiece point.   125

[Sound a flourish.] Enter Feliche.

PIERO.

What might import this flourish? Bring us word.

FELICHE.

Stand away. Here's such a company of flyboats hulling
about this galleas of greatness that there's no boarding him.
[*To* Piero.] Do you hear yon thing call'd, Duke?

PIERO.

How now, blunt Feliche; what's the news?   130

FELICHE.

Yonder's a knight hath brought Andrugio's head,
And craves admittance to your chair of state.

Cornets sound a sennet; enter Andrugio *in armor.*

PIERO.

Conduct him with attendance sumptuous,
Sound all the pleasing instruments of joy,
Make triumph, stand on tiptoe whilst we meet;   135
O sight most gracious, O revenge most sweet!

ANDRUGIO [*reading the letter*].

*We vow by the honor of our birth to recompense any man that
bringeth Andrugio's head with twenty thousand double pistolets and
the endearing to our choicest love.*

PIERO.

We still with most unmov'd resolve confirm   140
Our large munificence; and here breathe
A sad and solemn protestation:
When I recall this vow, O let our house
Be even commanded, stained and trampled on
As worthless rubbish of nobility.   145

ANDRUGIO.

Then here, Piero, is Andrugio's head   [*Raising his helmet.*]

140. resolve] *Bullen;* resolu'd *Q.*

---

125. *truss . . . point*] lace up the top of my codpiece; i.e., retire from the
amorous battle.
127. *flyboats*] small sailing vessels.
127. *hulling*] drifting.
128. *galleas*] large galley.   142. *sad*] serious.

Royally casqued in a helm of steel;
Give me thy love and take it. My dauntless soul
Hath that unbounded vigor in his spirits
That it can bear more rank indignity   150
With less impatience, than thy canker'd hate
Can sting and venom his untainted worth
With the most viperous sound of malice. Strike!
O, let no glimpse of honor light thy thoughts;
If there be any heat of royal breath   155
Creeping in thy veins, O stifle it.
Be still thyself, bloody and treacherous.
Fame not thy house with an admired act
Of princely pity. Piero, I am come
To soil thy house with an eternal blot   160
Of savage cruelty; strike, or bid me strike.
I pray my death, that thy ne'er-dying shame
Might live immortal to posterity.
Come, be a princely hangman, stop my breath.
O dread thou shame no more than I dread death.   165

PIERO.

We are amaz'd, our royal spirits numb'd
In stiff astonish'd wonder at thy prowess,
Most mighty, valiant and high-tow'ring heart.
We blush, and turn our hate upon ourselves
For hating such an unpeer'd excellence.   170
I joy my state, him whom I loath'd before
That now I honor, love, nay more, adore.

The still flutes sound a mournful sennet. Enter [Lucio *with*] *a coffin.*

But stay; what tragic spectacle appears?
Whose body bear you in that mournful hearse?

LUCIO.

The breathless trunk of young Antonio.   175

---

148. *it*] my head.
171–172. *I joy . . . adore*] It pleases my majesty that he whom I loathed
formerly, I now love.
172.1. *still flutes*] flutes with a soft tone.

MELLIDA.

    Antonio, ay me, my lord, my love, my—

ANDRUGIO.

    Sweet precious issue of most honor'd blood,
    Rich hope, ripe virtue, O untimely loss!
    [*To* Lucio.] Come hither friend; pray thee do not weep.
    Why, I am glad he's dead; he shall not see   180
    His father's vanquish'd by his enemy,
    Even in princely honor; nay, pray thee speak;
    How died the wretched boy?

LUCIO.

    My lord—

ANDRUGIO.

    I hope he died yet like my son, i' faith.   185

LUCIO.

    Alas, my lord.

ANDRUGIO.

    He died unforc'd, I trust, and valiantly?

LUCIO.

    Poor gentleman, being—

ANDRUGIO.

    Did his hand shake or his eye look dull,
    His thoughts reel, fearful, when he struck the stroke?   190
    And if they did, I'll rend them out the hearse,
    Rip up his cerecloth, mangle his bleak face,
    That when he comes to heaven the powers divine
    Shall ne'er take notice that he was my son.
    I'll quite disclaim his birth; nay, pray thee speak;   195
    And 'twere not hoop'd with steel, my breast would break.

MELLIDA.

    O that my spirit in a sigh could mount
    Into the sphere where thy sweet soul doth rest.

PIERO.

    O that my tears bedewing thy wan cheek
    Could make new spirit sprout in thy cold blood.   200

BALURDO.

    Verily, he looks as pitifully as a poor John; as I am true

---

192. *cerecloth*] shroud.
201. *poor John*] dried hake.

knight, I could weep like a ston'd horse.

ANDRUGIO [*to* Piero].

Villain, 'tis thou hast murder'd my son.
Thy unrelenting spirit, thou black dog,
That took'st no passion of his fatal love,   205
Hath forc'd him give his life untimely end.

PIERO.

O that my life, her love, my dearest blood,
Would but redeem one minute of his breath!

ANTONIO [*rising from the coffin*].

I seize that breath. Stand not amaz'd, great states;
I rise from death that never liv'd till now.   210
Piero, keep thy vow, and I enjoy
More unexpressed height of happiness
Than power of thought can reach; if not, lo, here
There stands my tomb and here a pleasing stage,
Most wish'd spectators of my tragedy;   215
To this end have I feign'd, that her fair eye
For whom I liv'd, might bless me ere I die.

MELLIDA.

Can breath depaint my unconceived thoughts?
Can words describe my infinite delight
Of seeing thee, my lord Antonio?   220
O no; conceit, breath, passion, words be dumb,
Whilst I instill the dew of my sweet bliss
In the soft pressure of a melting kiss:
Sic, sic, iuvat ire sub umbras.

PIERO.

Fair son—now I'll be proud to call thee son—   225
Enjoy me thus. [*Embraces* Antonio.] My very breast is thine;
Possess me freely; I am wholly thine.

ANTONIO.

Dear father.

---

202. *ston'd*] gelded.   205. *passion*] compassion.
209. *seize*] take legal possession.   209. *states*] princes.
210. *never liv'd*] never knew what life could mean.
212. *unexpressed*] unexpressible.
224. *Sic . . . umbras*] "Thus, thus it pleases (me) to descend into the
shades" (*Aeneid* iv. 660); cf. *Spanish Tragedy*, II.v.79.
225. *son*] son-in-law.

ANDRUGIO.

    Sweet son, sweet son; I can speak no more;

    My joy's passion flows above the shore   230

    And chokes the current of my speech.

PIERO.

    Young Florence prince, to you my lips must beg

    For a remittance of your interest.

GALEATZO.

    In your fair daughter? With all my thought.

    So help me, faith, the naked truth I'll unfold: 235

    He that was ne'er hot will soon be cold.

PIERO.

    No man else makes claim unto her?

MATZAGENTE.

    The valiant speak truth in brief: no.

BALURDO.

    Truly, for Sir Jeffrey Balurdo, he disclaims to have had

    anything in her.   240

PIERO.

    Then here I give her to Antonio.

    [*To* Andrugio.] Royal, valiant, most respected prince,

    Let's clip our hands. I'll thus observe my vow:

    I promis'd twenty thousand double pistolets

    With the endearing to my dearest love   245

    To him that brought thy head; thine be the gold,

    To solemnize our houses' unity.

    My love be thine, the all I have be thine.

    Fill us fresh wine, the form we'll take by this:

    We'll drink a health while they two sip a kiss.   250

    Now there remains no discord that can sound

    Harsh accents to the ear of our accord,

    So please you, niece, to match.

ROSSALINE.

    Troth, uncle, when my sweet-fac'd coz hath told me how

    she likes the thing call'd wedlock, maybe I'll take a survey 255

    of the check-roll of my servants; and he that hath the best

---

253. you] *Bullen;* your *Q.*

249. *form*] the formal ratification.
256. *check-roll*] list of servants.

parts of—I'll prick him down for my husband.

BALURDO.

For passion of love now, remember me to my mistress, Lady
Rossaline, when she is pricking down the good parts of her
servants. As I am true knight, I grow stiff; I shall carry it. 260

PIERO.

I will.

Sound Lydian wires; once make a pleasing note
On nectar streams of your sweet airs to float.

ANTONIO.

Here ends the comic crosses of true love;
O may the passage most successful prove.   265

                       [*Exeunt all save* Andrugio.]

FINIS.

---

262. *once*] once and for all.

Epilogus

[Andrugio comes forward for the Epilogue.]

Gentlemen, though I remain an armed Epilogue, I stand not
as a peremptory challenger of desert, either for him that
composed the comedy or for us that acted it, but a most
submissive suppliant for both. What imperfection you have
seen in us, leave with us and we'll amend it; what hath 5
pleased you, take with you and cherish it. You shall not be
more ready to embrace anything commendable than we will
endeavor to amend all things reprovable. What we are, is by
your favor. What we shall be, rests all in your applausive
encouragements.   *Exit.* 10

---

8. *What we are*] such success as we have at present.
9–10. *applausive encouragements*] encouragement by clapping your hands.

Appendix

Chronology

Approximate years are indicated by*, occurrences in doubt by (?).

Political and Literary Events	Life and Major Works of Marston
1558	
Accession of Queen Elizabeth.	
Robert Greene born.	
Thomas Kyd born.	
1560	
George Chapman born.	
1561	
Francis Bacon born.	
1564	
Shakespeare born.	
Christopher Marlowe born.	
1570	
Thomas Heywood born.*	
1572	
Thomas Dekker born.*	
John Donne born.	
Massacre of St. Bartholomew's Day.	
1573	
Ben Jonson born.*	
1576	
The Theatre, the first permanent public theater in London, established by James Burbage.	John Marston born, only son of lawyer John Marston and Marie Guarsi, of Italian extraction.
1577	
The Curtain theater opened.	
Holinshed's *Chronicles of England, Scotland and Ireland.*	
Drake begins circumnavigation of the earth; completed 1580.	

1578

John Lyly's *Euphues: The Anatomy of Wit.*

1579

John Fletcher born.

Sir Thomas North's translation of Plutarch's *Lives*

1580

Thomas Middleton born.

1583

Philip Massinger born.

1584

Francis Beaumont born.*

1586

Death of Sir Philip Sidney.

John Ford born.

1587

The Rose theater opened by Henslowe.

Marlowe's *TAMBURLAINE*, Part I.*

Execution of Mary, Queen of Scots.

Drake raids Cadiz.

1588

Defeat of the Spanish Armada.

Marlowe's *TAMBURLAINE*, Part II.*

1589

Greene's *FRIAR BACON AND FRIAR BUNGAY.*

Marlowe's *THE JEW OF MALTA.*

Kyd's *THE SPANISH TRAGEDY.*

1590

Spenser's *Faerie Queene* (Books I–III) published.

Sidney's *Arcadia* published.

Shakespeare's *HENRY VI*, Parts I–III,* *TITUS ANDRONICUS.*

1591

Shakespeare's *RICHARD III.*   Enters Brasenose College, Oxford (?).

1592

Marlowe's *DOCTOR FAUSTUS** and *EDWARD II.**
Shakespeare's *TAMING OF THE SHREW** and *THE COMEDY OF ERRORS.**
Death of Greene.

Matriculates at Brasenose College. Member of the Middle Temple, London.

1593

Shakespeare's *LOVE'S LABOUR'S LOST;* Venus and Adonis* published.
Death of Marlowe.
Theaters closed on account of plague.

1594

Shakespeare's *TWO GENTLE-MEN OF VERONA;* The Rape of Lucrece* published.
Shakespeare's company becomes Lord Chamberlain's Men.
James Shirtley born.*
Death of Kyd.

Graduates B.A.

1595

The Swan theater built.
Sidney's *Defense of Poesy* published.
Shakespeare's *ROMEO AND JULIET,* A MIDSUMMER NIGHT'S DREAM* RICHARD II.**
Raleigh's first expedition to Guiana.

Residing in the Middle Temple.

1596

Spenser's *Faerie Queene* (Books IV–VI) published.
Shakespeare's *MERCHANT OF VENICE,* KING JOHN.**

1597

Bacon's *Essays* (first edition).
Shakespeare's *HENRY IV*, Part I.*

1598

Demolition of The Theatre.
Shakespeare's *MUCH ADO ABOUT NOTHING,* HENRY IV*, Part II.*
Jonson's *EVERY MAN IN HIS HUMOR* (first version).

The Metamorphosis of Pygmalion's Image and *The Scourge of Villainy.*

Seven books of Chapman's translation of Homer's *Iliad* published.

1599

The Paul's Boys reopen their theater.

HISTRIOMASTIX,* *ANTONIO AND MELLIDA,** Parts I and II.

The Globe theater opened.

Shakespeare's *AS YOU LIKE IT,** *HENRY V, JULIUS CAESAR.**

Dekker's *THE SHOEMAKER'S HOLIDAY.**

Death of Spenser.

1600

Shakespeare's *TWELFTH NIGHT.**

JACK DRUM'S ENTERTAINMENT.*

The Fortune theater built by Alleyn.

The Children of the Chapel begin to play at the Blackfriars.

1601

Shakespeare's *HAMLET,** *MERRY WIVES OF WINDSOR.**

WHAT YOU WILL,* *SATIROMASTIX* (?) (with Dekker).*

Insurrection and execution of the Earl of Essex.

Jonson's *POETASTER* (ridiculing Marston).

1602

Shakespeare's *TROILUS AND CRESSIDA.**

1603

Death of Queen Elizabeth; accession of James VI of Scotland as James I.

Florio's translation of Montaigne's *Essays* published.

Shakespeare's *ALL'S WELL THAT ENDS WELL.**

Heywood's *A WOMAN KILLED WITH KINDNESS.*

Shakespeare's company becomes the King's Men.

THE MALCONTENT* (played by the Queen's Revels company of boys, at the Blackfriars—a company in which Marston had acquired shares; stolen and acted by the King's Men at the Globe).

1604

Shakespeare's *MEASURE FOR MEASURE,** *OTHELLO.**

Chapman's *BUSSY D'AMBOIS.**

THE FAWN,* *THE DUTCH COURTESAN.**

1605

Shakespeare's *KING LEAR.**
Bacon's *Advancement of Learning*
published.
The Gunpowder Plot.

1606

Shakespeare's *MACBETH.**
Jonson's *VOLPONE.**
Tourneur's *REVENGER'S TRAG-
EDY.**
The Red Bull theater built.
Death of John Lyly.

1607

Shakespeare's *ANTONY AND
CLEOPATRA.**
Beaumont's *KNIGHT OF THE
BURNING PESTLE.**
Settlement of Jamestown, Virginia.

1608

Shakespeare's *CORIOLANUS,**
*TIMON OF ATHENS,** *PERI-
CLES.**
Chapman's *CONSPIRACY AND
TRAGEDY OF CHARLES, DUKE
OF BYRON.**
Dekker's *Gull's Hornbook* published.
Richard Burbage leases Blackfriars
Theatre for King's company.
John Milton born.

1609

Shakespeare's *CYMBELINE;** *Son-
nets* published.
Jonson's *EPICOENE.*

1610

Jonson's *ALCHEMIST.*
Chapman's *REVENGE OF BUSSY
D'AMBOIS.**
Richard Crashaw born.

1611

Authorized (King James) Version
of the Bible published.
Shakespeare's *THE WINTER'S
TALE,** *THE TEMPEST.**

*EASTWARD HO** (with Jonson and
Chapman).
Marries Mary Wilkes of Bradford,
Wilts.

*SOPHONISBA.**
The City Pageant.

The Ashby Entertainment.
*THE INSATIATE COUNTESS**
(completed by William Barksted).

Committed to Newgate prison by
the Privy Council (for reasons
unknown).

Ordained deacon and then priest.

Beaumont and Fletcher's *A KING AND NO KING*.

Tourneur's *ATHEIST'S TRAGEDY*.*

Chapman's translation of *Iliad* completed.

1612

Webster's *THE WHITE DEVIL*.*

1613

The Globe theater burned.

Shakespeare's *HENRY VIII* (with Fletcher).

Webster's *THE DUCHESS OF MALFI*.*

Middleton's *A CHASTE MAID IN CHEAPSIDE*.

Sir Thomas Overbury murdered.

1614

The Globe theater rebuilt.

The Hope Theatre built.

Jonson's *BARTHOLOMEW FAIR*.

1616

Publication of Folio edition of Jonson's *Works*.   Vicar of Christchurch, Hants.

Chapman's *Whole Works of Homer*.

Death of Shakespeare.

Death of Beaumont.

1618

Outbreak of Thirty Years War.

Execution of Raleigh.

1620

Pilgrim Fathers land at Plymouth.

1621

Middleton's *WOMEN BEWARE WOMEN*.*

Robert Burton's *Anatomy of Melancholy* published.

Andrew Marvell born.

1622

Middleton and Rowley's *THE CHANGELING*.*

Henry Vaughan born.

1623
Publication of Folio edition of Shakespeare's *COMEDIES, HIS-TORIES, AND TRAGEDIES*.
1625
Death of King James I; accession of Charles I.
Death of Fletcher.
1626
Death of Tourneur.
Death of Bacon.
1627
Death of Middleton.
1628
Ford's *THE LOVER'S MELAN-CHOLY*.
Petition of Right.
Buckingham assassinated.
1631
Shirley's *THE TRAITOR*.   Resigns his living of Christchurch.
Death of Donne.
John Dryden born.
1632
Massinger's *THE CITY MADAM*.*
1633
Donne's *Poems* published.   Marston's *Works* published.
Death of George Herbert.
1634
Death of Chapman, Webster.*   Death of Marston.
THE TWO NOBLE KINSMEN
(with title-page ascriptions to Shakespeare and Fletcher) published.
Milton's *Comus*.
1635
Sir Thomas Browne's *Religio Medici*.
1637
Death of Jonson.
1639
First Bishops' War.
Death of Carew.*
1640
Short Parliament.

Long Parliament impeaches Laud.
Death of Massinger, Burton.

1641
Irish rebel.
Death of Heywood.

1642
Charles I leaves London; Civil War breaks out.
Shirley's *COURT SECRET*.
All theaters closed by Act of Parliament.

1643
Parliament swears to the Solemn League and Covenant.

1645
Ordinance for New Model Army enacted.

1646
End of First Civil War.

1647
Army occupies London.
Charles I forms alliance with Scots.
Beaumont and Fletcher First Folio published.